LANGUAGE AND LITERACY SERIES

Dorothy S. Strickland, FOUNDING EDITOR
Celia Genishi and Donna E. Alvermann, SERIES EDITORS

ADVISORY BOARD: Richard Allington, Kathryn Au, Bernice Cullinan, Colette Daiute, Anne Haas Dyson, Carole Edelsky, Shirley Brice Heath, Connie Juel, Susan Lytle, Timothy Shanahan

---

* Volumes with an asterisk following the title are a part of the NCRLL set: Approaches to Language and Literacy Research, edited by JoBeth Allen and Donna E. Alvermann.

(Continued)

Literacy Tools in the Classroom

*Teaching Through Critical Inquiry,
Grades 5–12*

*Richard Beach
Gerald Campano
Brian Edmiston
Melissa Borgmann*

foreword by
Jerome C. Harste

Teachers College
Columbia University
New York and London

The National Writing Project
Berkeley, CA

Published simultaneously by Teachers College Press, 1234 Amsterdam Avenue, New York, NY 10027 and the National Writing Project, 2105 Bancroft Way Berkeley, CA 94720-1042

The National Writing Project (NWP) is a professional development network of more than 200 university-based sites, serving teachers across disciplines and at all levels, early childhood through university. The NWP focuses the knowledge, expertise, and leadership of our nation's educators on sustained efforts to improve writing and learning for all learners.

The authors wish to express gratitude for permission to use the following:

"March for Me," by Tish Jones. Copyright © 2009 by Tish Jones. Published by permission. (Used in Chapter 6.)

"Honoring Student Stories," by Gerald Campano. In *Educational Leadership*, 2007, 65(2), pp. 52–54. Copyright © 2007 by ASCD. Reprinted with permission. Learn more about ASCD at www.ascd.org. (Used in Chapter 4.)

Library of Congress Cataloging-in-Publication Data

Literacy tools in the classroom : teaching through critical inquiry, grades 5–12 / Richard Beach . . . [et al.] ; foreword by Jerome C. Harste.
    p. cm. — (Language and literacy series)
  Includes bibliographical references and index.
  ISBN 978-0-8077-5056-8 (pbk. : alk. paper) — ISBN 978-0-8077-5057-5 (hardcover : alk. paper) 1. Language arts (Secondary) 2. Language arts (Elementary) 3. Inquiry-based learning. I. Beach, Richard.
  LB1631.L445 2010
  428.0071--dc22

        2009051827

ISBN 978-0-8077-5056-8 (paperback)
ISBN 978-0-8077-5057-5 (hardcover)

Contents

Foreword

The function of a foreword, like the function of curriculum, is to give perspective. As someone interested in both the arts and critical literacy, I found that this volume fills an important need. As I write this foreword, I'm involved in a 2-week institute on "Literacies and Difference" in which I am doing a workshop entitled "Using the Arts to Make Our Classrooms Critical." I wish that this volume were already in publication. I would be using it. It is a well-thought-out answer to the question I am constantly asked by teachers: "What does critical literacy mean in terms of what I might consider doing differently in my classroom?" And in terms of my workshop, "How might the arts be used to productively support students in taking on a critical stance?" The authors of this volume, Richard Beach, Gerald Campano, Brian Edmiston, and Melissa Borgmann would find, by the way, these questions from teachers problematic; in light of all the territory they cover in this book, they also want us to rethink the traditional relationship between theory and practice. Their goal in this regard is twofold: to develop practical theory as well as theoretical practice.

Critical literacy is about unpacking the systems of meaning that are operating in society to position us. From a curricular perspective, critical literacy involves disrupting the commonplace, interrogating multiple perspectives, focusing on the sociopolitical, and taking social action. In their attempt to support teachers and students in taking on a critical literacy perspective, Beach, Campano, Edmiston, and Borgmann demonstrate how various tools might be used in various classroom and content areas to support inquiry, agency, identity, and space. The tools they talk about span all of the expression of language (reading, writing, speaking, and listening) as well as art (visual literacy), music, drama, and digital literacy. Through the framework of inquiry, agency, identity, and space, they expand current definitions of language as well as how the language arts potentially might operate across the curriculum. When seen as tools, the humanities suddenly constitute a communication potential as well as a vehicle for creating a very different kind of literate being.

I see curriculum as a metaphor for the lives we wish to live and the people we wish to be. The initial chapters support readers in getting their heads around critical literacy and how curriculum might be used to address issues of social significance to today's students. The rest of the chapters demonstrate how this is possible across the curriculum using what I call the arts as tools. I love the fact that they describe real classroom settings and tell real classroom stories. I also love the fact that they *build* curriculum *from* children rather than *do* curriculum *to* children. By privileging student identities they disrupt extant notions of curriculum as a course to be run and focus it instead on issues that disrupt normativity. Their curriculum is critical and intent on preparing students to understand and use literacy to transform their worlds. In summary, these authors retheorize education in light of the experiential background of today's youth. The engagement begins in the personal, ends in the social, and in the process lays bare the literacy practices that define today's youth as well as the literacy practices that they might use to reposition themselves in the world.

While most books ask middle school and high school teachers to take the content presented and adapt it to the middle school and high school classroom, *Literacy Tools in the Classroom: Teaching Through Critical Inquiry, Grades 5–12* applies to other grades. This does not mean that the book should not be used with elementary preservice and inservice teachers. But elementary teachers will have to take these literacy tools and adapt them to their grade level. Turnabout, I think, is fair play and really quite easy, as ideas jump out at you as you read the text. I say this as an elementary teacher and as one whose focus has always been elementary education. I firmly believe, as do these authors, that quality instructional engagements focus on underlying fundamental processes in language and literacy learning. This is why the book is appropriate up and down the curriculum and with audiences beyond the ones being directly addressed.

Teachers will love the fact that the book ends with a chapter on assessment. Again the authors are edgy, asking us to not just count or attend to what is easy but to focus on what really matters. In some ways "what really matters" is the theme of the whole book. The authors ask us to think about literacy practices as mattering, curriculum practices as mattering, and teaching practices as mattering, all in light of the kind of literate world we wish to create and the kind of critically literate people we want our students to be.

Jerome C. Harste

Introduction

Many of the students enrolled at Roosevelt High School, Minneapolis, Minnesota, were simply not engaged with their academic curriculum. They saw little purpose in instruction focusing primarily on preparing them to pass standardized reading/writing tests and were subsequently dropping out of school, channeling their creative and intellectual energies elsewhere. One of their English teachers, Delainia Haug, who taught media studies and digital production, was well aware of these students' dilemma. She understood why they would develop an oppositional stance toward a school curriculum that seemed to lack meaning and relevance. At the same time, she recognized that dropping out was not the answer. Dropping out would most likely further limit the students' life opportunities, many of whom were already growing up in contexts of poverty and class segregation.

So Delainia decided to take action. She believed in the potential of digital literacy tools to both engage students and provide them with opportunities to put academic skills in the service of self-determination and empowerment. However, her school owned few computers, and students had limited computer access in their homes. And while she was promoting technology in her own classroom, students received very little digital support across their other courses.

Given these challenges, Delainia and her colleagues, along with faculty from the University of Minnesota, created a Digital Media (DigMe) program within her school. In this program, students in English, social studies, science, and mathematics employ digital media literacy tools such as blogs, wikis, digital photography/video, GPS devices, and podcasts to partake in a range of interdisciplinary projects (Cormany, 2009). For example, students work in teams to map the cultural geography of their city in a social studies class, take digital photos of their neighborhoods with Delainia, and analyze the local water quality in science. Students then use their creations to produce online audiovisual productions documenting issues facing their neighborhoods. The program staff also applied for support to purchase new computers and iPods so that students had increased access to digital literacies in their classrooms, as well as technical support from the district.

1

(For a description of the program see http://www1.umn.edu/news/features/
UR_CONTENT_097501.html.)

Through their participation in the program, the students began to experience an increased sense of agency. To share their work and promote
their program, they produced podcasts, wikis, a school newspaper, a school
Web site for social networking (http://teddies.ning.com), and digital videos
(http://tinyurl.com/n2sbnv). Using these different digital literacy tools allowed students to display competence to their peers, teachers, and community, enhancing their engagement with school and confidence in their ability
to communicate their ideas to multiple audiences.

Delainia's experience represents a major redefinition of literacy instruction, one that moves beyond resistance to digital literacies by adopting a
"parallel pedagogy" that integrates both print and digital literacies (Leander,
2009). We wrote this book to share stories like this, in which educators are
actively engaging their students in the use of literacy tools to enhance learning in all subject-matter areas. Rather than conceive of literacy as simply a
set of skills to be acquired, we perceive the DigMe students as using literacies as *tools* for both responding to and producing texts for the purposes
of critiquing the status quo and creating new collaborative spaces and roles
for themselves. In the process, they also achieved a sense of agency. The students became public intellectuals—ethnographers, scientists, documentary
filmmakers, environmentalists, community activists, and journalists—who
were making a difference in their own lives as well as the lives of others.
The literacy tools we feature in this book can support all students to achieve
the same.

PERSPECTIVES INFORMING THIS BOOK

In this book, we demonstrate that literacy tools can be used to engage students in critical inquiry, help students create spaces for learning, enact more
empowering identities, and establish their sense of agency through making
change. We build this literacy curriculum framework drawing on a number
of different theoretical perspectives:

- From sociocultural/activity theory learning theorists' (Cole, 1996;
  Engestrom, 1987; Sannino, Daniels, & Gutiérrez, 2009; Wertsch,
  1998) notion of tools as mediating means to achieve purposes or as
  objects driving participation in activities. For example, narratives
  can be used as tools to entertain, describe an event, illustrate

a point, pay tribute to someone, unearth a buried history, link subjective experience to more comprehensive knowledge about the world, or navigate a difficult situation. Teaching effective use of these tools therefore involves designing activities by modeling the functions of narrative and encouraging students to practice using it to achieve various purposes.

- From "new literacy" learning theory (Corio, Knobel, Lankshear, & Leu, 2008; Freire & Macedo, 1987; Gee, 1996, 2004; Knobel, 1999; Street, 1984, 1995), we derived the key idea of literacy as inherently social—as involving ways of connecting with others to construct, co-create, and redefine identities, as reflected in the DigMe students' uses of literacy tools to collaborate with one another and inform audiences outside their school.

- From critical literacy/inquiry theory (Beach & Myers, 2001; Cochran-Smith & Lytle, 2009; Dozier, Johnston, & Rogers, 2005; Lewison, Leland, & Harste, 2008; Luke & Freebody, 1997; Morrell, 2008; Wells, 1999), we perceive literacy tools as a way to theorize practice, investigate power and inequality, and promote liberation.

- From digital literacy theorists (Jenkins, 2006; Kress, 2003; Lankshear & Knobel, 2006), we perceive the need to provide students with the kinds of technologies students were using in the DigMe program that are central to networked participation in the knowledge economy, as well as going beyond a focus only on print-based reading and writing instruction to include a range of different audio, visual, and digital media to communicate ideas.

- From process drama, hip-hop, and performance theories (Alim, 2006; Chang, 2005; Edmiston, 2008; Edmiston & Enciso, 2003; Fisher, 2005, 2007; Goffman, 1959; Heathcote & Bolton, 1995; O'Neill, 1995; Schneider, Crumpler, & Rogers, 2006), we perceive that literacy tools such as dramatic inquiry and spoken-word poetry provide students with a sense of voice through improvised social interactions and the possibility of shaping understanding through the use of social imagination to explore ideas from multiple perspectives.

- From realist theories of experience (Alcoff, 2005; Mohanty, 1997; Moya, 2001; Teuton, 2008), we view students' individual and collective identities as sources of knowledge, joy, and political solidarity.

- Finally, we draw on third-generation assessment theorists (Carr, 2001; James et al., 2006; Lewis, 2008; Swaffield, 2008) in

moving away from traditional testing regimes that were leading
the Roosevelt students to drop out to use of more meaningful
assessments that foster student self-reflection and inquiry about
their proficiency in using literacy tools to achieve change in lived-
world contexts.

Our understanding of literacy tools is also based on decades of experience
working directly with students and teachers in our varied capacities as teachers, educational activists, and teacher educators. We have adopted a critical
inquiry stance in our own work by continually interrogating problems in the
status quo and envisioning alternatives (Cochran-Smith & Lytle, 2009).

In describing specific examples of tool use, we also draw on our own
research studies, observations, and student interviews in grade 5–12 classrooms. Each chapter contains examples reflecting a diverse range of students and educational contexts.

THEORIZING FROM PRACTICE: SUMMARIZING THE CHAPTERS

In the first section of the book we elaborate on our conceptual framework
by describing how actual students and teachers have used literacy tools to
achieve certain purposes leading to change and growth. Chapter 1 describes
how a historical figure, Frederick Douglass, and a contemporary person,
Maribel, employ literacy tools to resist institutional racism in the past and
present. We share these stories as a way of introducing our conceptual model of tool use with respect to its interrelated purposes of inquiry, space,
identity, and agency. Chapter 2 focuses on critical inquiry and space. We
describe how literacy tools, such as Critical Response Protocol question-
asking, may foster inquiry through the creation of alternative intellectual,
material, and social spaces. Chapter 3 focuses on the purposes of enacting
identity and establishing agency through displays of competence in using
literacy tools.

The next section goes into detail about uses of specific literacy tools.
Chapter 4 explores the role of narrative in the literacy curriculum. We describe how stories can be used to excavate histories and experiences buried
in the regular school curriculum. We make an argument for the need to
honor student stories and suggest that although student narratives are often personal, they may also contribute more generally to our shared understandings of the world. Chapter 5 describes the use of dramatic inquiry as
a literacy tool for engaging students in imagining and understanding issues
from multiple perspectives as well as for extending agency and developing

identities. Chapter 6 focuses on students' use of spoken-word poetry performances to voice their experiences to audiences. We learn how Tish Jones and other founding members of the performance art collective Teens Rock the Mic used spoken-word poetry as performance artists and community activists to expose injustice and productively leverage power for positive change. Chapter 7 describes how digital literacy tools support students' collaborative process of mutual communication and shared knowledge construction through online role-plays, blog posts, wikis, and podcasts. Chapter 8 examines uses of reflective writing, including freewriting, note-taking, and fieldnotes for thinking and organizing experience. Chapter 9 demonstrates how students respond to and create images and videos to critically inquire into issues such as the social significance of skin color and physical appearance.

Finally, Chapter 10 picks up on the idea of change-based assessment introduced in Chapter 3 by providing specific criteria to evaluate students' growth over time based on their abilities to use literacy tools in projects of change and transformation. We believe that the ultimate criteria for evaluating the effectiveness of and students' competence with literacy tools should come from the testimonials and self-reflections of the students themselves. In this spirit, we share longitudinal case studies of several young people, introduced early in the book, who are now older and have themselves become community educators who inspire future generations.

THE WIKI RESOURCE SITE

In addition to the material in this book, we provide related links, examples of student work, teaching activities, and further reading for each chapter on a wiki resource site: http://literacytooluses.pbworks.com. We will be continually updating this wiki and also invite readers to add their own links, student work, lesson plans, and further reading suggestions. To add material by editing pages (please do not delete material), readers simply need to have a pbworks.com account; questions about editing can be addressed to Richard at rbeach@umn.edu.

HOW EDUCATORS CAN USE THIS BOOK

Our aspirations for this book are that grade 5–12 teachers in all content areas:

- *View current sociocultural, critical literacy learning theory and classroom practice as mutually informing.* While this book focuses on grade 5–12 classrooms, we believe educators across all levels and subject-matter areas—from pre-K to university—can be inspired by the examples in this book to work together to create richer, more equitable literacy curricula.

- *Develop purpose-driven activities or projects.* The descriptions of teachers' and students' uses of literacy tools reveal potential uses of a wide array of literacy tools for socially just purposes.
- *Recognize ways in which literacy tools can be an avenue to develop and showcase students' strengths.* Students develop a positive cycle, in which exposure to and engagement with literacy tools allows them to hone their skills and experience success, which in turn motivates further engagement.
- *Foster learning across the content areas.* Literacy tools are not solely appropriate in the English/language arts classroom, but can inform learning across the curriculum. This book provides rich examples of students taking up literacy tools for interdisciplinary inquiry.
- *Devise specific criteria for providing feedback.* Students and teachers reflect on the tools and develop their own criteria as to whether they've effectively met goals.

ACKNOWLEDGMENTS

We would also like to acknowledge our Teachers College Press editors—Meg Lemke, Judy Berman, and Aureliano Vázquez Jr.—and Maria Paula Ghiso for all of their help in assisting us in making this book a reality.

ONE

What Are Literacy Tools and How Can We Use Them?

Moving Legacies into the 21st Century

The master's tools will never dismantle the master's house.
—Audre Lorde, *Sister Outsider*, p. 112

We have been motivated to write this book by feelings of possibility and of urgency. The possibility has been buoyed by our writing during an election season, which reminds us of the ongoing necessity to retain hope and continue to strive for much-needed social change. We have witnessed renewed civic awareness and commitment to equity in the face of challenging economic, political, and human rights issues. As educators in the research and practitioner communities, we are presented with a window of opportunity to imagine literacy teaching, learning, and professional development differently.

We feel a sense of urgency because although there are many powerful counterexamples to the predominant mode of teaching literacy (a number of which will be documented in this book), in a widespread sense there has been very little change in how literacy is taught in public schools. This inertia is articulated plainly and eloquently by Morton Botel, professor emeritus at the University of Pennsylvania and past president of the International Reading Association. In a document entitled "An open letter to all those who may influence the new educational policies of federal, state and local governments," Botel (2008) recounts how, over the past 4 decades, "Washington has spent hundreds of billions of dollars almost entirely on improving children's achievement on the 'basic skills' as measured by standardized tests. And where are we? Students' performance nationally plotted over that long stretch looks essentially like a flat line while their graduation rates are steeply declining." After 40 years and almost unimaginable spending—including financial windfalls for the testing industry and textbook companies that have capitalized on remediation, scripted teaching, and assessments—nothing has really changed. The high-stakes testing paradigm rolls along unabated.

It is important to note that Botel is neither a partisan participant in the "reading wars" nor an armchair critical pedagogue and provocateur. He is recognized as a temperate and judicious scholar with a historic sense of the field as well as deep and sustained experience working on the ground with teachers and school districts both nationally and internationally. In the letter he continues to explain that according to every "statistical expert" it is fundamentally invalid and unreliable to use standardized tests for "'diagnosing and prescribing' curriculum and instruction. . . . Yet that's how standardized tests have been used since the 1960's with the advocacy of federal mandates from the Right to Read in the 1970's to the current No Child Left Behind." Despite evidence to the contrary from cross-disciplinary meta-research and the protestations of almost every single national professional organization, the federal government has persisted in endorsing what Botel labels an "anti-intellectual and unproductive instructional framework" that emphasizes so-called basic skills and, we might add, the instrumental quantifying of ability and sorting of students.

The result has been a remedial and deficit-based approach to teaching that has attenuated any rigorous curriculum that might promote "reasoning logically, thinking critically and creatively, thinking analytically and synthetically, posing and solving problems, communicating, collaborating and reflecting"—the "super skills of the 21st Century." In this case, it may not be too cynical to suggest that though the literacy curriculum has functioned as a tool, it has been a tool in the service of social reproduction rather than equity and empowerment. It is the most underresourced schools and vulnerable students who are being denied rich literacy experiences in schools. The arts have mostly gone by the wayside, especially in many Title 1 schools. So has much attention to fundamental values that give teaching and learning meaning: ethics, aesthetics, social justice. An innovative literary curriculum also entails a cosmopolitan view of citizenship that resists reducing schooling to the individualistic ability to compete, by following an ideal articulated by Susan Sontag (2008), the "extension of sympathies to other selves, other domains, other dreams, other worlds, other territories." We would do well to view all students as global intellectuals.

At this point the consequences of our archaic curricular paradigm are undeniable: The opportunity gap remains as intractable as ever, high school dropout rates are an unconscionable embarrassment, students are disengaged from school literacy, and many teachers are demoralized. We offer *Literacy Tools in the Classroom* to those educators interested in building more intellectually rigorous and equitable literacy learning environments conducive to the fuller flourishing of all students' academic and creative potentials. We believe a broader understanding of literacy will enable students to develop a more participatory and potentially more liberatory relationship to the world. While we hope for more auspicious policy conditions, we realize that real transformation ultimately is energized from below. In this time of aspirations for change, we turn to those who are committed to envisioning and bringing into reality educational frameworks that are more commensurate with the forms of knowledge and sophisticated literacy practices of robustly diverse 21st-century students.

"THE RAFT IS NOT THE SHORE": HONORING OUR LITERATE LEGACIES

The literacy tools descibed in this book are not necessarily all that new. While we will be introducing many cutting-edge ways in which literacy use has been extended by technology and the arts to create innovative opportunities for learning, we situate this work within historical and community legacies of literacy, social resistance, and cultural transformation. We want to acknowledge that contemporary progressive educators are the heirs to the visions, struggles, and sacrifices of many others who have put literacy tools in the service of making differences in their own and others' lives. Following Thich Nhat Hanh's (Hanh & Berrigan, 2000) endorsement of spiritual pluralism, we understand literacy tools not as ends in themselves— "the raft"—but as means to create emancipatory pedagogical projects. This should be the true destination, the shore, of our work.

We illustrate this larger vision of tool use through two stories of transformative literacy: a brief discussion of the life of Frederick Douglass and a more extended account of the migrant narrative of a contemporary young Quechua woman. The first is one of the most iconic representations in the American literary canon of the relationship between literacy and freedom. The second is a contemporary story of a complex and difficult journey that is at once unique as well as representative of how many put language and literacy in the service of greater self-determination. Both examples, we believe, illustrate how agents individually and collectively strive to use literacy as a tool to alter their life trajectories and build more empowering futures for themselves and subsequent generations, often at great peril, loss, and pain. These narratives also speak to the profound critically literate legacies of resistance and hope many of our students inherit from their families and communities, legacies, we will suggest, that are often not honored and sometimes explicitly devalued in schools.

Frederick Douglass's intellectual, spiritual, and physical journey to free-dom and his account of self-transformation through literacy is rightly can-onized. He was born into slavery in Maryland and famously learned to read at the age of 12, despite strict laws forbidding the schooling of slaves for fear it could foment rebellion. Douglass in fact honed his understandings of human rights and freedom by reading *The Columbus Orator* and would go on to teach other slaves how to read at a Sabbath School on his plantation. Scholars of critical pedagogy (e.g., Cutter, 1996) have contributed to our understandings of the significance of Douglass's narrative by noting that it is not a "mere celebration of literacy." The acquisition of reading skills in and of itself did not lead to Douglass's fundamental self-transformation, even though gaining access to the written word was an unequivocal act of courage, resistance, and agency. Equally important was how Douglass used literacy as a tool to dismantle oppression. For example, he made incisive in-terpretations of the Bible and of the Constitution that exposed the hypocrisy of slavery and undermined its justification.

Douglass (1986) himself famously asserted in his autobiography that "you have seen how a man was made a slave; you shall see how a slave was made a man" (p. 107). The powerful symmetry of his prose asserts fundamental human capacities—such as the ability for all people to criti-cally discern their environment and act toward greater freedom—that are necessary for any argument for universal rights. While abolitionists may have presented Douglass's virtuosic literary and oratory skills as evidence of a slave's humanity, Douglass himself claimed a categorical humanity prior to their acquisition. Douglass's quote more specifically suggests the role that literacy may play in both the making and unmaking of slavery. From the lens of contemporary literacy theory, Douglass might be considered a constructivist: He demonstrated that the identities of slaves and slave own-ers were constituted, in part, through language, and that there are no such things as purely "oral" or "literate" cultures or minds that possess funda-mentally different cognitive capacities as suggested by anthropologists such as Walter Ong (Ong, 1982). There are, rather, multiple literacies that must be understood within specific contexts. As Houston Baker (1980) observed, *The Narrative Life of Frederick Douglass* reflects his rhetorical use of the "linguis-tic codes, literary conventions, and audience expectations" of his times, as his work and literate practices drew from a range of cultural and discursive resources, from his African inheritance to the literacy codes of the white su-premacist slave society into which he was born. Unlike more skeptical strands of constructivism, however, Douglass might not subscribe to a relativistic view of language, where discourse presents only different versions of reality. He spoke of "freedom" and the "power of truth." It is easy to imagine that he believed language could be used to build a freer and more just world.

A little over a century and a half after Frederick Douglass penned his autobiography, a young woman named Maribel (pseudonym) crossed the Rio Grande River between Texas and Mexico. The geographical and auto-biographical details of Maribel's experiences we share below are a composite of different border-crossing stories that were shared with Gerald, although they mostly come from one particular person; this decision was made in order to protect any individual's identity. Following Nobel Prize–winner and indigenous rights activist Rigoberta Menchú, we also view this narrative as not belonging only to one individual, but as the story of a people. However, it is also important to note that this account, if anything, underestimates the perils and challenges conveyed in the oral narratives.

Maribel was weary, not only for having run 3 hours straight through deserted areas, thorns, trees, wires, and sewage, but also because her journey didn't just begin in Mexico. It had begun 3 months earlier, in the Andes, and involved the crisscrossing of numerous political borders and cultural boundaries, including those between Peru and Brazil, Brazil and Bolivia, and Bolivia and Paraguay.

At one point in the desert, just shy of the river, Maribel collapsed from exhaustion. In retrospect, she didn't know how she was able to get up and keep going, except for the knowledge that she had to. After waiting for several more hours in the brush, Maribel and the young men accompanying her (she was the only female in the group) were given the signal to go because the water had calmed and the authorities seemed to have passed. The river was broad, murky, and littered with debris. Maribel had to wade through the water so as not to draw the attention of vigilantes with guns and flashlights, who could be heard laughing in the distance. Her feet barely touched the river bottom and the water would periodically flush her nose and clog her throat. She strenuously held a plastic bag with dry clothes above her head, which would come in useful on the other side. Thirty minutes later, on U.S. territory, she changed and continued to run. Although scared, stumbling, and longing to stop for good, she was grateful not to be in Arizona, where the desert is hotter, the distances longer, and a group had recently been discovered dead from dehydration. After 2 more hours, Maribel found sanctuary in a house, where she stayed underground for 2 weeks. She eventually passed the final checkpoint stowed away in a compartment in the bed of a truck, covered with lemon juice to keep sniffing dogs at bay.

Although Maribel had crossed several borders, making it to Mexico was a particularly important step, and not only because it was near her final

destination. If at this point the authorities caught her, there was a possibility she would only be returned to a border town if she could convince the
border patrol that she was Mexican, rather than all the way to her country
of origin, where she would have to start her journey from zero. Every delay
was extremely costly, in terms of both psychic energy and the rapidly dimin-
ishing funds that had been pooled and saved for years and across generations. The organizers of the trip had been up front that there are no guaran-
tees and that they could control for only about 20% of the circumstances.
As for the remaining 80%, well, the saying is "Go with God": some kind of
mysterious admixture of luck, possibly fate, and individual agency.

It is in the portion of the migration that may be attributed to agency
where we can begin to understand Maribel's border crossings as a complex
and studied literate negotiation: or, building off Heath, a performative and
high-risk literacy event. In Heath's (1983) well-known formulation, a literacy event is defined as "any occasion in which a piece of writing is integral
to the nature of participants' interactions and their interpretive processes"
(p. 93). Several pieces of writing informed the event of the border encounter.
Maribel's "homework"—work that would literally help her and the daughter she carried in her womb gain access to a safer and more secure home—
included studying books about Mexican food and history, memorizing the
national anthem, and practicing regional dialects and vocabulary.

Maribel's journey also included performative elements. Erving Goffman
(1959) characterizes a performance as an "activity of a given occasion
which serves to influence in any way any of the other participants" (p. 15).
For example, Maribel had to be prepared to convince border patrol agents
that she had lost her identification and that she was indeed a Mexican citizen, a form of rhetorical passing perhaps reminiscent of the Underground
Railroad. Finally, the literacy event of the border crossing may be qualified
as high-risk because it occurred within conditions of stark power asymme-
try. Several of the border patrol agents at previous crossings were cruel, and
there were severe consequences if this one did not go well, including possible
imprisonment, and deportation to a life of constant economic struggle, if
not abject poverty.

On what sociolinguists call a local and "microgenetic" (Wortham,
2005) scale, one attentive to present interaction, Maribel's journey and border crossings are a clear example of self-respectful and informed literate
agency, reflecting her ability to critically read her conditions and act toward
greater freedom. In a matter of weeks, days, and even seconds, Maribel's
identity as well as life circumstances could suddenly change. However, it is
important to understand the moment of border crossing not merely as an
individual choice isolated in time.

To gain a clearer sense of the tensions between structure and agency and the determinants that constrain Maribel's choices, it is also worth considering the gravity of the literacy event from a historical perspective. Maribel was compelled to migrate because of global economic forces that have, over decades, eroded opportunities for sustainable livelihood in her native country. She described her decision to come to the United States as a need, not a luxury, albeit one fueled by a media-induced romance with New York City. Her move was also part of a historical pattern. Maribel's parents themselves had been forced to flee violence and poverty in their indigenous mountain village and subsequently adapt to local cultural prejudices in order to survive. As they grew older, without adequate resources and health care, Maribel felt an obligation to them, as well as to her own future children, to seek a better life. The choice to migrate was nevertheless painful. She knew that if she left she would rarely or possibly never see her parents and many relatives again. Her future daughter would mark the first generation in a thousand years not to hear the accents of her community's native Quechua language (an indigenous language of Peru) at home and, unless she had the fortune of attending a bilingual school, it was probable that her family's Spanish would be compromised as well. These realities weighed heavily on her decision.

What role will language and literacy play in mediating Maribel's relationship to the new spaces in her life? One of the defining characteristics of the migrant and refugee experience may be the impossibility of ever really finding a safe and secure home. The second she set foot in her new country Maribel would become the recipient of what Denny Taylor (1996) might call a particularly "toxic" form of literacy: social ascription and categorization. She was instantly labeled as "undocumented," "illegal," and a potential "felon," despite the obvious irony and hypocrisy of applying these categories to a member of an indigenous community, whose people have the most historic claims to the continent and who have been subject to repeated forms of illegal colonization and subjugation themselves. These ascriptions not only stigmatize the circumstances of birth and social location, but also attempt to restore an idealized and exclusionary notion of nationhood and community, which is reinforced through literacy policies such as English-only laws. It would be insufficient, however, to understand Maribel's identity solely in terms of institutional naming and interpellation; they do not "exhaust" a person. The moment of border crossing was for Maribel an unremarkable reality and danger, and one of many necessary moves of survival and self-definition. And in her ongoing process of survival and becoming, multiple literacies play an invaluable role.

The stories of Maribel and Frederick Douglass, and many others that inform our teaching and research, have helped us recognize that people learn to use literacy tools to enact and change their identities as well as society, as they, like our own students, move on rafts into new, uncharted territories. This led us to formulate an alternative instructional framework and define a set of literacy tools that work to "dismantle" dominant educational approaches that do a disservice to students as well as help teachers build curricular experiences that will tap into the rich legacies of students in diverse 21st-century classrooms. Each of the chapters of this book explores these literacy tools in depth, providing their theoretical underpinnings as well as concrete examples of how actual educators have used these tools to create meaningful and engaging learning experiences.

DEFINING LITERACY TOOLS

It is in reflecting on these examples that we can define precisely what we mean by literacy tools. As many educational researchers have emphasized, literacy cannot be reduced to the acquisition of individual tasks, such as reading the newspaper, completing an application, or taking an exam. Brian Street (1984) challenged such "autonomous" conceptions of literacy as a collection of neutral skills, noting that all literacy practices are inherently "ideological": intimately related to cultural and social contexts and their power dynamics. A singular literacy is replaced by multiple literacies (Street, 1995); as such, there are many different ways to be literate, but some have more capital in schools than others. A "critical" approach to literacy is one that makes contesting worldviews visible (Luke & Freebody, 1997).

Literacy tools include any artifact, idea, or process that people use when they read and write or otherwise use language to make meaning. We understand texts as extending beyond print to include digital, visual, audio, and performed texts. We view individuals and groups as agents who use literacy tools in the service of transformation. Literacy is neither static nor detached from social situations; as such, literacy learning necessarily entails developing the ability to use literacy tools to transform relationships, spaces, the focus of people's inquiry, and identities.

In the sense that we desire change that creates more equitable relationships and lives, we take a social justice perspective on transformative literacy. Both Douglass and Maribel employed literacy to achieve specific transformative purposes (Cole, 1996; Wertsch, 1998). For Douglass, learning to read and write was not an end in itself, a matter of acquiring a decontextualized skill. He developed and used his abilities of interpretation, authorship, and oratory to expose the hypocrisy of and contradictions in Judeo-

Christian apologias for slavery and make profound human rights claims. Maribel's literate performances were in the service of survival, enabling her to transverse political borders, inhabit new cultural spaces, and make more stable accommodations for herself and her family. The story of her journey, her migrant narrative, also potentially conveys an ethical and political message. In the tradition of the Latin American testimonial, her use of story as a literacy tool invites listeners to situate her experiences and identity within personal and collective struggles for humanization.

This purposeful nature of language and literacy is a fundamental tenet of Cultural-Historical Activity Theory (Engestrom, 1987; Sannino, Daniels, & Gutiérrez, 2009), which analyzes human tool use and agency within a network of relations and in a learning community constituted by a distribution and division of intellectual and material labor. In and of themselves, tools are just tools; a hammer by itself is just a hammer. An apprentice learns to use a hammer for specific ends—to drive in nails, help construct a home for Habitat for Humanity, or refurbish a historic landmark. The hammer mediates one's relationship to an object as part of a transformative project. Similarly, language and literacy are tools that mediate the relationship between students and purposes, including the interpretation and composition of texts. The use of language and literacy as tools happens across the life span and levels of social organization, from the young child beginning to use words to reason and accomplish tasks, as in Vygotsky's (1967) famous account of language development, to youth activists exploiting online venues to agitate for change, to larger institutional committees and working groups developing bureaucratic codes and policies. In all cases, there is a dialectical relationship between individuals and the larger social and cultural contexts.

Literacy learning best occurs when students are engaged in meaningful activities that have authentic purposes. This may seem obvious. But as we have already stressed, literacy policy has been geared toward the teaching of reading and writing as a discrete set of skills that can be transmitted and, in isolation, shorn from any substantive creative and dynamic context. For example, many tests that students take in schools have no analogy in the world outside the test-taking situation. Their purpose is only to reify a top-down "accountability" system that sorts students and schools along limited and socially damaging criteria of "success" or "failure." We were reminded of this type of tautological rationale—students must train for the tests because they are a reality—by an English professor at an elite Ivy League university, who lamented that over the years the freshman composition skills have degraded. His comment wasn't a curmudgeonly evaluation of youth today, but rather a critique of an educational system that had conditioned students to view writing as a formulaic exercise conducted during a 45-minute period on an arbitrary topic. What becomes lost is the art of the literary essay, a tool—one of many—for reflection, investigation, and critical interpretation. The professor was speaking in reference to highly "successful" students—a cohort that had learned to navigate the educational system and master its power codes. Lamentably, we have also seen how the current drill-and-assessment paradigm has further marginalized students who are most vulnerable in schools due to the indignities of tracking, poor resources, and low expectations. It is no surprise that so many young people are disenchanted with schooling and dropping out, choosing instead to channel their creative and intellectual energies into out-of-school venues and learning communities.

LITERACY TOOLS FOR PROJECTS OF CHANGE
AND TRANSFORMATION

In this book we provide a number of powerful examples of how literacy tools have been taken up in educational contexts as divergent as an elementary school in Columbus, Ohio, and some in-school digital media programs in both an urban and a suburban high school in the Minneapolis, Minnesota, area, as well as a public K–6 all-boys academy in northwest Indiana, and an ethnically and linguistically diverse neighborhood school in California's Central Valley. We try to provide as many concrete examples of teacher activities and student work as possible to demonstrate the need to think about the use of literacy tools as embedded within visionary projects of change and transformation of both status quo systems and students' sense of agency.

There is always the concern that any literacy tool—no matter how innovative—may be appropriated for the very agendas that have been doing a disservice to student learning and empowerment. For this reason, we define the purposes of tools more expansively, to include not merely the instrumental mastery or acquisition of discrete skills or access to new technologies, but also as intimately tied to achieving four basic purposes: engaging in critical inquiry, creating spaces, enacting identities, and establishing a sense of agency. In Chapters 2 and 3, we elaborate in more detail on these four purposes.

We offer the following interrelated purposes for the use of literacy tools in order to build a case for "change-based assessment," in which the ultimate value of a tool rests on its effectiveness in identifying (and posing) problems and envisioning alternatives for equity and justice.

Purpose 1: Engaging in Critical Inquiry: Using Literacy Tools to Construct Knowledge

From a Freirian (1986) perspective, all students are critical and dialogic generators of knowledge despite systems that position them as passive recipients of information. We believe that one devastating and long-term effect of colonization and oppression is a crisis of epistemic authority: members of historically marginalized communities are taught that their ways of knowing are somehow less worthy, more mired in conditions of social and cultural deprivation (Lee, 2007). There are many contemporary manifestations of this form of supremacy in education, including widespread educational assumptions and professional development programs that propagate the stereotypes that students labeled as "LD" require "special" (i.e., more prescriptive) education or that "children in poverty" are somehow cognitively deficient and think "less abstractly" than their peers because of how they are raised (e.g., see Osei-Kofi's [2005] incisive critique of Ruby Payne). Any equitable pedagogical relationship has to be based on the fundamental theoretical premise that all students are intellectuals whose diverse social locations afford them "privileged" epistemic access to the world, including insights into how it is unjust and how it might be improved (Campano, 2007; Moya, 2001).

We therefore align ourselves with those who argue that literacy tools should be embedded in critical and dialogic inquiry-based approaches to teaching and learning (Cochran-Smith & Lytle, 2009; Lewison, Leland, & Harste, 2008; Morrell, 2008; Wells, 1999), where communities of learners not only gain expertise with actual tools, but also use them to investigate knowledge, build interpretations, and formulate understandings about the world, including how society might be more equitably organized and their role in such transformations. Frederick Douglass's access to literacy enabled him to turn the justifications for slavery against themselves. Similarly, students will be particularly motivated to use tools to construct knowledge if that knowledge has relevance to their lives.

Purpose 2: Creating Spaces: Using Literacy Tools to Co-Construct and Inhabit Contexts

As young people use the various literacy tools we describe, they transform their spaces for lived experiences and learning. We believe that when students and teachers have greater freedom to shape classroom environments and social relationships, these material and relational alterations make possible different ways of knowing. When we "spatialize" our thinking about literacy learning (Leander & Sheehy, 2004), we recognize how classroom organizational structures and social interactions (e.g., moving the chairs into a circle for a discussion, laying out materials to paint a class mural, enabling students to participate in online discussions, or performing ideas) are material and social manifestations of a more equitable distribution of intellectual authority among the classroom community.

Out-of-school contexts often provide a venue for students' multiliteracies, which are many times marginalized in traditional classroom arrangements. For example, members of Anakbayan-USA, a youth group dedicated to seeing the linkages between the minoritized experiences of Filipina/os in America with human rights issues back home, use digital media to create and sustain transnational activist communities. Although this work requires significant social organizing and analysis, it would most likely be outside the purview of the regular curriculum. Youths' digital competencies illustrate the frequent mismatch between home and school literate practices (Knobel, 1999; Taylor, 1996) and the role of social and cultural "funds of knowledge" in mediating school interactions (Gonzalez, Moll, & Amanti, 2005; Velez-Ibanez & Greenberg, 1992). How students approach literacy activities and create and use texts may be different in the "first" spaces of school than in out-of-school "second" spaces; however, using a range of literacy tools may enable teachers to create hybrid "third spaces" (Gutiérrez, Baquedano-López, & Turner, 1997) that are attuned to the fuller range of students' experiential worlds.

There is also a "politics of place": how the ability to access and navigate spaces is often a matter of power. Douglass's Sabbath School classroom constituted a profound space of resistance to White Southern hegemony. Maribel's ability to navigate the spaces in her life will affect her quality of life and that of her child. If she is fortunate to encounter teachers who value her daughter's multicultural and multilingual identity, the classroom third space may be enriched by her heritage. If a student mural project is begun where Maribel lives, the neighborhood may reclaim its community space.

Purpose 3: Enacting Identities—Using Literacy Tools to Author a Personal and Collective Sense of Self

We cannot embed the use of literacy tools in projects of change and transformation without acknowledging the epistemic significance of identities. So much of the great progress over the past centuries with respect to justice and equity is the direct result of identity-based social movements, including the African American, feminist, labor, immigrant, and indigenous civil and human rights movements. It may be well worth reiterating that the changes and insights derived from these grassroots and popular struggles do not merely benefit particular groups, but all of humanity, and invaluably contribute to our shared knowledge base. Similarly, we view the rich diversity of 21st-century classrooms as a profound opportunity for personal and collective intellectual and ethical growth, rather than as a "problem," as it is too often framed.

The philosopher Linda Martin Alcoff (2005) argues that social identities are "real" and "fundamental to the self" as well as "relational" and "contextual" (p. 90). We form our identities through others. But there are also real consequences—both positive and negative—to these relational ascriptions that shape the ways in which individuals interpret and navigate their social environments. It has become something of a reflex in the literacy field to suggest that identities are elastic categories and social constructions and to note the (often deterministic) role that language and discourse play in creating and enforcing difference. What perhaps has been less emphasized is how identities are not merely social constructions; they may also be conceptual lenses through which to more accurately "read" and ultimately engage the world, an insight perhaps most powerfully and eloquently theorized by members of the Future of Minority Studies (FMS) interdisciplinary research project at five different universities (site for Stanford University: http://ccsre .stanford.edu/RI_rp_FutureMinor.htm). This realist theory understanding of identities reminds us that they "have causal determinacy over our epistemic and political orientations to the world—what we notice, what we care about—but also . . . profoundly affect how we are seen and interacted with by others." One important implication of this understanding is that individuals who occupy subjugated or marginalized social locations may have privileged epistemic insight into how the world operates to sustain suffering and inequality.

By defining one of the goals of literacy tools as enacting identities, we hope to highlight how students from diverse backgrounds may employ tools to mobilize their experiential and cultural resources. That is, student (and teacher) identities are potentially a useful construct for generating knowledge and forming positive intellectual and social bonds, not just a negative "effect" of discourse and language. We are also endorsing the idea that education can fundamentally matter in people's lives and that literacy can potentially transform one's self-understanding and, subsequently, understanding of others and the world.

Purpose 4: Establishing Agency—Using Literacy Tools to Read, Act In, and Change the World

The ineluctable twinning of knowledge and power is one of the most important contributions of modern social theory. Maribel's example demonstrates the ways in which literacy is a fulcrum for power, enabling agents to shape life possibilities and reconfigure the conceptual, emotional, social, and material landscape. Similar to Douglass, Maribel's narrative recounts an act of freedom and also contributes to a larger counterdiscourse about what it means to be a hemispheric American and a world citizen deserving of fundamental human rights.

As educators concerned with student growth, it is not enough to stop at the insight that neither knowledge nor language are neutral. We must also recognize that language and literacy practices are underwritten by power relationships, values, and contesting worldviews that can and should be normatively evaluated. As Orwell (1948) famously observed, there are ways in which words can obscure reality, such as in the distorting and dehumanizing euphemistic language of war and torture—"enhanced interrogation techniques" is a well-noted contemporary example.

In the educational world, there is a proliferation of labels that put students in boxes, often circumscribing their experiences. At the same time, language can also be used to name unfairness on the playground or injustice in the community and to provide contextually richer and more comprehensive and accurate accounts of human potentials. Language may also promote healing and understanding. Maribel's poignant and informative story is a stark contrast to the "impersonal" and often dehumanizing representations of human suffering found in both common public discourse and in academic literature about migration (Mills, 2009). In this sense, Maribel's literate practices both exemplifies and enacts agency.

We believe that literacy tools may promote agency by enabling students to both "read their worlds" (Freire, 1970/2000) accurately and empower themselves to make critically autonomous decisions. This may occur in a classroom interaction, where a child previously labeled as "at-risk" or "troublesome" engages in dramatic play or performance to reposition himself as talented and capable. Or students may take collective action outside the classroom, for example, by creating a documentary on police brutality in the neighborhood.

Literacy pedagogy based on an understanding of student agency within critical and dialogic inquiry will invariably involve a degree of conflict (Moya, 2001). Students and teachers may not just become proficient at using tools in order to apprentice or assimilate into a "community of practice" (Wenger, 1998). Rather, when lives within and beyond classrooms are viewed as "contact zones" (Pratt, 1991), teachers can promote "communication across lines of difference and hierarchy that go beyond politeness but maintain mutual respect" (p. 38). Such transformational framing may be socially imagined as part of dramatic inquiry or through the analysis of everyday realities and perspectives. Young people may then employ literacy tools to critique limitations of the status quo by "stepping outside one's usual mode of perception and comprehension using new frames to understand experience" (Lewison, Leland, & Harste, 2008, p. 8).

THE ART OF TEACHING AND CHANGE-BASED ASSESSMENT

As illustrated in Figure 1.1, these four purposes driving uses of literacy tools exist in a synergistic relationship and, we believe, are all necessary for projects of change and transformation.

For example, a student may investigate the history of Atzlán and the Treaty of Guadalupe Hidalgo using online resources to supplement the official version of history presented in the textbooks (inquiry). This knowledge may spur him to embrace his Chicana/o roots (identity), which will, in turn,

Figure 1.1. Four Purposes for Uses of Literacy Tools

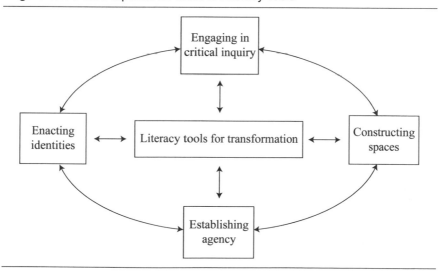

enable him to understand differently the experiences of many of his peers who are new to the country and thus shape his student identity. He may then decide to organize a letter-writing campaign (agency) in an after-school program (space) to support the legislation providing increased college scholarships for minority students. Similarly, through her students' narratives, a teacher may gain a deeper understanding of the experiences of her migrant families. This may help her cultivate more progressive White and teacher identities and begin to situate her cultural work as an educator in solidarity with the immigrant rights movement. She may subsequently reorient the curricula to critically examine exclusionary and racialized notions of nationhood and citizenship.

Any one of the purposes may be an entry point for a project of change and transformation and may be emphasized in varying degrees during any particular learning experience. In a rich literacy curriculum, there will most likely be a number of purposes being simultaneously forwarded, and, as the arrows signify, there is no linear trajectory for how this should happen, although there may be better and worse approaches in any given situation. The purposes are not mutually exclusive. Coming to political consciousness about one's personal experiences, for example, may be a requisite for taking action. There will also be specific considerations regarding which literacy tools would be appropriate for mediating the different purposes and tasks.

Each tool has particular affordances and constraints, and they can take on ideological meaning in the sense delineated by Street (1984, 1995): the work they do can only be understood within local social and cultural contexts. For example, Melissa (Chapter 2) describes how learning the literacy tool of question-asking helps students in a transformed classroom space to interrogate texts and their lives. In his work, Gerald and a co-teacher, Angelica, employed drama with a diverse group of fifth graders as a literacy tool to create a performative representation of the injustices in their own schooling. The collective and improvisational process of composing, enacting, and interpreting the multilingual dramatic performance, inspired by El Teatro Campesino, also challenged the school's own predominant ideology of individual authorship and evaluation to present an imagined alternative future vision (Medina & Campano, 2007).

To add another layer of deliberation, a learning community must not only think about which tools would be suited for a project of change, but also about how various literacy tools may function in concert to create multimodal representations of student inquiries. One powerful example is students combining personal narratives with visual images in processes of digital storytelling (Ohler, 2007). The complexity of this type of creative and intellectual work cannot be learned prescriptively, but only arrived at by educators who adopt an inquiry stance into their own practice. It is part of the art of teaching.

Like most heuristics, Figure 1.1 is not meant to be taken too literally. The purposes do not occupy discrete conceptual realms; they overlap. We hope the diagram will be a useful tool itself for reflecting on and assessing the literacy curriculum and both student and teacher learning. This form of change-based assessment may happen on both the collective and individual level through focusing on the effectiveness in using literacy tools to affect change. In a change-based assessment model, the students are evaluated by more than simply the intrinsic features of their work, but rather by the extent to which their work results in perceived, anticipated, and actual changes (Beach & Doerr-Stevens, 2009).

On the collective level, teachers may use the different purposes identified in Figure 1.1 to step back and collaboratively reflect on their teaching:

- Uses of literacy tools to engage in critical inquiry, for example, identifying challenges facing students' neighborhoods, leading to change in students' level of civic participation.
- Participation in physical and virtual spaces within the school to share their ideas, for example, on ways to address issues facing neighborhoods, leading to change in the level of students' willingness to voice their ideas.
- Uses of literacy tools to enact alternative identities, for example, identities of being "active citizens" in their neighborhoods.
- Establishment of a sense of agency, for example, to create a neighborhood Web site to make change in their neighborhood.
- Changes in their uses of literacy tools over time, including reflecting on changes using "learning stories" (Carr, 2008) and e-portfolios. If students, for example, are creating a digital map to examine issues of environmental injustice in their neighborhood, this inquiry will require a range of literacy practices drawing on students' diverse social and cultural resources. Students could reflect on how their map led to changes in their ability to address environmental issues in their neighborhood.

As we describe in more detail in Chapter 10, rather than simply assessing students only on their literary proficiency, a change-based approach assesses students on their ability to use literacy tools to cultivate their beliefs, identities, and communities.

FROM PAST TO FUTURE USES OF LITERACY TOOLS

As we write this volume, Maribel's daughter is about to enter school for the first time. When she does, she will bring with her the legacies of Frederick Douglass, of her mother, of indigenous rights activists, and of so many other ordinary people who historically have struggled for educational progress and change. She will also be in the company of her peers, who will have their own signature stories and family histories. We are concerned that the literacy curriculum will marshal conformity and build walls to keep these legacies at bay. Yet there is also another possibility: that Maribel's sacrifices will be honored in her daughter's education—and that of all young people—through an inclusive and intellectually robust curriculum that reveres students' diverse identities, worlds, and capacities to generate knowledge and make positive changes in the world. We hope the tools highlighted in this book will be useful to educators committed to this enlarged vision of literacy learning.

TWO

How Do We Use Literacy Tools to Engage in Critical Inquiry and Create Spaces?

Knowing about the world involves knowing how to change it.
—Satya Mohanty, *Literary Theory*, p. 10

The teachers in this book turn toward, and embrace, the collective minds, hearts, energies, and imaginations of the students in their classrooms by grappling with engaging questions and pressing problems that lead to social justice–oriented inquiries and actions. They believe that the literacy tools of talking, reading, writing, and the arts are best used collectively and critically to create spaces where students can make a difference in the world by promoting more fairness and equity.

In this chapter, we focus on two of our four purposes for using literacy tools (see Figure 1.1): engaging in critical inquiry and creating spaces. We endorse a view of inquiry as "stance" (Cochran-Smith & Lytle, 2009), a theoretical orientation where "practice is not simply instrumental in the sense of getting something done, but also and more importantly, it is social and political in the sense of deliberating what is to be done, why to get it done, who decides, and whose interests are served" (p. 121). Jerry Harste (2001) gives a compelling argument for why he believes "education is inquiry and inquiry is education," how critical inquiry is "a new way of conceptualizing schooling," and why "we need to give [young people of all ages] tools with which they can outgrow us and yet help themselves" (p. 1):

> As I see it, all we guarantee the students we teach is that they will face problems of some magnitude and that no single individual is going to be able to fix the problems. If the messes we hand future generations are to be resolved, I suggest that it will take a lot of good minds that know how to learn and how to collaborate. (p. 2)

An inquiry stance brings critical inquiry into the everyday life of the classroom as people collaboratively explore and seek to understand and redress whatever current problems are pressing for them or for people they care about. Inquiry becomes *critical* in spaces where young people, working alongside supportive adults, begin to "question the everyday world and consider actions that can be taken to promote social justice" (Lewison, Leland, & Harste, 2008), especially in interrogating beliefs and attitudes. And, as Gerald has argued (Campano, 2009), inquiry also needs to go beyond critique. It is also a form of pedagogy where students and teachers are creating alternative educational spaces more conducive to fuller human flourishing. Critical inquiry creates spaces where people of all ages can grow, raise questions, and make a difference in their own lives and the lives of others.

CRITICAL INQUIRY LITERACY TOOLS

In the summer of 2002, a group of Minneapolis teachers, including Melissa, met to reflect about their work in the previous school year at Minneapolis North Community High School, a school located in a diverse urban neighborhood: 80% of North High School students receive free and reduced lunch, 47% graduate, and the mobility rate is 50%. The group addressed critical inquiry questions such as "How do our exterior landscapes reflect and impact our interior spaces?," "How is art a representation of identity?," "How is art political?," and "How are strengths born from experience?," questions that drove the North High students' work in writing, art, dance, and spoken-word poetry. While the students were producing rich and provocative work, this collaborative team still found themselves asking, "So what? To what end? What next? Had anything shifted or been transformed?" Students were still dropping out, teachers were still burning out, and the community still suffered from poverty and unemployment.

This led the group to address a new critical inquiry question, "What does it take for communities to thrive?" Melissa had her own working response to this question:

> For me to thrive as an individual, I need to tell stories of how I got here. I need to be seen, or have my gifts acknowledged and used for some purpose greater than myself. I wonder what it would look like if all people were seen or acknowledged in a community? What if all were viewed as possessing gifts—and these gifts were recognized and used toward some greater end? What if all people could tell their stories? And what if we really listened? Would that be enough? More than enough? Would there be less crime, more peace? What would be created? What would be sustained?

Using the Critical Response Protocol

Posing such questions as part of their own critical inquiry about the challenges faced in their school led these teachers to formulate some critical inquiry questions for their students to employ in the classroom. And for Melissa, these discussions resulted in her use of the Critical Response Protocol (CRP) as a critical inquiry literacy tool, a tool originally used by Liz Lerman (Lerman & Borstel, 2007) to provide feedback for dance artists.

Melissa uses the CRP as a pedagogy to engage students in critical inquiry by inviting them to formulate open-ended questions based on noticing, reminding, feeling, wondering, and learning about images, texts, phenomena, or experiences. Students begin by asking each other: "What are you noticing?" This encourages others to attend to specific details or aspects of a statement, claim, or image they are studying. Participants in the facilitated protocol experience describe what they see or hear, deferring judgment about the "text" before them. Whenever a statement is made that lacks specificity or reveals a value-laden assertion, the clarifying question is posed, "What did you see that makes you say that?"

The second question is, "What does it remind you of?" Students make intertextual connections among what they notice about images, texts, and phenomena and their own lived experiences or other prior knowledge. This is an essential part of engaging the community of participants. The shared stories and references builds what Carol D. Lee (2007) refers to as "cultural data sets" that recognize the lived experiences of all learners, and simultaneously that knowledge has cultural roots beyond any one teacher's complete familiarity (Gadsden, Davis, & Artiles, 2009). Melissa describes this as the "dendrite-building" phase of the process, as it helps make associations that reinforce learning and retention.

The third question identifies emotions, answering the query, "How do you feel?" This involves risk-taking and trust and fosters community-building, as students identify how a text has the power to trigger emotion, which in turn leads to further introspection: "What questions does the 'text' raise for you? What did you learn?" These questions can lead to identifying and contextualizing issues, problems, and topics in other texts and experiences, and empower learners in their own construction of knowledge.

It is important that teachers using the CRP continually attend to, and reflect, on students' questions and answers in order to provide support, as well as model the approach for students who have difficulty posing questions. As Melissa poses the CRP questions, inviting her students to facilitate this process for themselves and for one another, they learn to apply them as heuristics for critical thinking and analysis. Students move away from the assumption that there are "right answers" when they hear a variety of different responses being perceived as valid by the teacher. Using these questions also slows students down to meditate and observe what is before them; they defer judgments while collaboratively constructing knowledge through critical inquiry.

As students use CRP to make connections—identifying emotions, asking questions, and speculating on the intention of an author—this process can ultimately lead to performing understandings of a text (Wiggins & McTighe, 2005). For example, in reading Zora Neale Hurston's (1937/1991) *Their Eyes Were Watching God*, Melissa's 12th grade English students Shaina and Shavon (pseudonyms) were drawn by the idea that Hurston's central character, Janie, is a dreamer, a young woman seeking love and discovering more about herself in the process. They connected passages from Hurston's work with Alicia Keys's song "Caged Bird" to write their own song illustrating their comprehension and interpretation of Janie's journey in self-knowledge, self-love, and self-awareness. The juxtaposition of Hurston's text alongside Key's lyrics, coupled with Shaina and Shavon's own personal experiences and emotions around love, lead them to pose questions like: "Who is Janie? Who are we? How do we understand her? How are we connected? What does it mean to be caged? What does it mean to be free?"

These questions became the inspiration for their engagement with, and making meaning of, Hurston's text as they co-wrote an original song entitled "I'm a Dreamer," which they subsequently performed for their peers. In their collaborative performance of the work, they reveal a larger lesson about the interconnectedness of life and humanity. Their performance demonstrated their understanding of Hurston's novel, as well as a dimension of their identities that the girls amplified when they created buttons they wore to class that read simply, "I am Janie."

To support students in asking generative questions, Melissa has them form a circle and suggests that they listen to questions before immediately proposing answers. For example, in one of her classes, students posed the following questions:

Why can't people overcome fears? Where did everything begin? Can we all just get along? Am I ready? Can suffering bring you pleasure? Why does she do this to herself? Can pleasure cause you to suffer? Do emotions speak louder than words? Or do words speak louder than emotions when it comes to love? Why do people make bad choices? Why are innocent children killed by hunger and war? What is evil? How did your name come about? What puts one human above another? Why do people put each other down? What is the price of one life? How does home impact who you are? What comes first in society—morals or law? How does the way you were raised affect who you are? Why can't people accept failure?

Students then reflect on the process of question-asking itself in terms of how posing questions helps them develop ideas for writing. Students note that while questions are useful for thinking further about a topic or issue, once they begin to generate answers they need to use those answers to identify further problems and formulate possible solutions in a systematic manner. To do so, they use their answers in problem/solution reports organized according to statements of problems, reasons for problems, possible solutions, and reasons those solutions may work.

Students can also use CRP to analyze and dramatize current events. For example, in one urban 9th-grade English classroom in 2006 the teacher, Angela Lynsky, was active in the Save Darfur Campaign. Brian found that after viewing a 10-minute home video on YouTube about Darfur posted by an anonymous student elsewhere, along with a short CNN clip of refugees receiving food, the students' responses and thus their inquiry questions were quite varied. While all agreed on a purpose (to stop the genocide in which an estimated 1 million people had died) and most wanted to act and "do something," there was disagreement in a heated discussion about the best tools to use: letters, advertising at a car wash, meeting with the principal, or phone calls to politicians' aides were all discussed. Some students were concerned that other people, like the president, should act, arguing that whatever they did as young people wouldn't make a difference. While some thought only changing the situation in the refugee camps in Darfur would stop genocide, others thought that action in the school would be worthwhile. Their analysis shaped their debate about the effectiveness of different actions and strategies, ranging from a short-term local information campaign in the school to letter-writing to influencing longer-term international action through the United Nations.

One way to navigate competing framings and avoid unproductive arguments is to reach agreement on a broad inquiry question, for example, "What might different people do to try to stop the killing in Darfur?" and then to explore the topic from different viewpoints that highlight competing dimensions and interpretations. Dramatizing events moves verbal debates and generalizing statements into the presentation and analysis of specific acts in particular scenes performed by actual people using different tools of agency to achieve their intended purpose. In the high school classroom, through dramatic improvisation students experienced and interpreted not only events they could do as young people, for example talking with the principal, but also events that only others could do, for example talking with their senator or going to Darfur as journalists.

Adopting a Critical Inquiry Stance

Using question-asking as a critical inquiry literacy tool, as with CRP, involves adopting a stance of not only posing questions, but also identifying specific problems and entertaining possible solutions. Cochran-Smith and Lytle (2009) characterize this stance as a process of "building, interrogating, elaborating, and critiquing conceptual frameworks that link action and problem-posing to the immediate context as well as larger social, cultural, and political issues" (pp. 51–52).

Adopting a critical inquiry stance also involves engaging in dialogue with others, and collective action leading to change. Making change requires convincing others of the gravity of a problem and the need for change, leading to involvement of more people willing to participate in collective, organized actions (Freire, 1970/2000). Schools often encourage students to voice their personal opinions about ways to improve their school, yet students can reasonably assume that even if they acted, as individuals they may lack power to make meaningful changes (Robinson & Taylor, 2007). However, by working with others, students gain verification for and confidence in voicing their opinions and ideas. Valerie Kinloch (2005) cites the example of a student, Jackie, who read aloud a poem she was writing:

> "Writing is a means of expression/ Expression is a way to get and remain/in conversation with oneself/It is,/in fact,/a way to be sane in a world of terror, greed, and war/But is it really democratic/to speak of writing, expression, terror, greed, and war/at the same time? Do I/have a right/to speak?"
>
> After reading her writing, I asked Jackie to share it with the class, and she did. The results were amazing: One student, using his Spanish language before translating his ideas into English, said he feels the same way—not poor and not disadvantaged, but afraid. Someone else talked about his brother being unfairly tracked into slow-paced classrooms; another student raised the issue of power and access; a final student asked the student near the back of the room what his name was—she had forgotten it, marked him as invisible, but now wanted to know, to remember. (p. 109)

This story suggests the value of having students work together in posing questions to identify problems and formulate possible solutions. Such collaboration is more likely to occur if the school curriculum is built around shared interdisciplinary inquiry.

Organizing a Critical Inquiry Curriculum

Critical inquiry can be used to organize the curriculum by focusing on the problems and questions raised about any issue. When students explore problems, approached as located in cultural institutions and social relationships that can always be considered from multiple competing perspectives, inquiry takes a critical turn. By asking broad inquiry questions as well as more specific related questions, students collaboratively explore and seek answers to their concerns about any topic or work of literature through informal investigations or more systematic research.

For example, the 10th-grade Biology, Language Arts, and Social Studies interdisciplinary curriculum at Nathan Hale High School, in Seattle, Washington, (http://www.seattleschools.org/schools/hale/reform/is/is_web/hale_integratedstudies3.html) is organized around the central question, alluding to Gandhi, "How can we be the change we want to see in the world?" In one unit, in order to study the political, economic, social/cultural, and technological causes and effects of epidemics on society, students address the question, "What happens when a system is changed?" In a second unit, students address the big question, "What are the costs and benefits of change and progress?" by studying changes in technology at the end of the 19th century, based on the personal question, "Do you think that this technology has benefited society?" In another unit, students study community members who make changes benefiting others. And in a fourth unit, the group dramatizes a mock trial based on the actions of characters in the novel *Lord of the Flies* (Golding, 1959) to address the question, "What is human nature? Can it or should it be changed?"

Throughout these units, students pose questions about their work based on "five habits of mind." These are 1) Evidence: "How do we know what's true and false? What evidence counts? How sure can we be?" 2) Connection: "Is there a pattern? Have we seen something like this before?" 3) Supposing: "Could it have been otherwise? What would happen if . . . ?" 4) Significance: "Why does it matter? Who cares about this?" and 5) Viewpoint: "What if we were looking at it from a different direction? What if we had different expectations?" These questions invite students to engage in critical thinking, analysis, and perspective-taking. For example, in responding to *Lord of the Flies* via a mock trial, students considered a larger question: Do the characters' actions represent humans' inherent evil nature? The charge was bolstered by those students who cited consistent patterns in characters' actions suggesting that they were evil. At the same time, this charge was countered by others' evidence that the characters were too young to know what they were doing.

Question-asking can be applied to current issues in social studies classes. In his 9th-grade social studies class at Roosevelt High School in Minneapolis, Minnesota, John Wood's students addressed the issue of urban sprawl in relation to the question, "What are the forces creating urban sprawl?" Students identified various forces: the availability of inexpensive land and housing in areas around cities, the decline in family farms, a preference for cars and highways over mass transit, and so on. They noted the problems created by urban sprawl: destruction of the environment and farmland, increased reliance on cars and highways, creation of pollution, tax burdens on outlying suburbs, and so forth. In posing and pursuing questions, the students were engaged in "disrupting the commonplace" (Lewison, Leland, & Haste, 2008, p. 7), not only to recognize that something is "just not right" about urban sprawl, but also to identify reasons for sprawl and the negative effects on cities.

To synthesize and present ideas, students used ComicLife software (http://plasq.com/comiclife) to create comics featuring the adventures of "StupidGrowthMan" and "SmartGrowthMan." Students' illustrations addressed the inquiry questions "Who are you and what do you do?," "What growth is coming to the Twin Cities?," "What can be good about growth?," and "What can be bad about growth?" Students studied examples of how other cities were addressing sprawl, creating comic illustrations of Portland, Oregon's urban growth boundary beyond which there can be no additional sprawl; Toronto's downtown housing developments, built to encourage an influx of residents to the area; and Atlanta's increased transit options and biking/walking paths. Students' comics were evaluated in terms of how they demonstrated an understanding of the effects of growth and urban sprawl in the Twin Cities and other cities, as well as what worked in Portland, Toronto, and Atlanta that could be applied to the Twin Cities.

To implement a critical inquiry curriculum, teachers involve students in the following activities, though they may not necessarily occur in this order (Beach & Myers, 2001):

- Identifying burning issues facing a group, community, city, society, and so on, or portrayed in a text that they care about, for example, the issue of the lack of alternative mass transit or bicycle lanes in their neighborhood.

- Formulating specific questions to drive inquiry related to tensions/ contradictions associated with these issues: different reasons for problems, how issues/problems are represented or framed, different possible resolutions, and reasons why solutions may or may not work to change the status quo. For example, what competing proposals or responses have been already been made and how do they frame the issues?
- Gathering information, data, or visual documentation that address these questions; critiques status-quo perceptions of the issues; explores alternative dimensions, for example, the amount of funding for mass transit or bicycle lanes versus the budget for automobiles; gathering views by interviewing local people; or taking photographs to create a slide show.
- Synthesizing and presenting reports about an issue not only to peers and teachers, but also to other audiences coping with the issue, for example, planning a school meeting, preparing for a public assembly with citizens, or contacting aides to arrange face-to-face interviews with elected officials.
- Reflecting on what was learned about the values and challenges of engaging in critical inquiry.

A critical inquiry stance toward curriculum study involves continually posing and exploring questions about texts, issues, and experiences. It is a process that reveals new views and new ideas that when turned into social actions transforms relationships, shape spaces, and thus change how students experience, understand, and act in the world of the classroom and beyond the walls of the school.

USING LITERACY TOOLS TO CREATE SPACES

We now turn to a second use of literacy tools—the creation of spaces. Spaces are more than physical sites. By *spaces*, we mean the evolving socially created and experienced cultural events and contexts that over time form and shape the different and often overlapping "worlds" that people of all ages inhabit and move among—community meetings, mealtimes, games of sport, celebrations, sales transactions, online chats, ceremonies, shopping malls, shared journeys, classrooms, and so forth.

Spatializing our approach to education highlights that learning is shaped by our actual lived social experiences and the literacy tools we use (Leander & Sheahy, 2004). Lefebvre (1991) theorizes that life is lived, experienced, and understood in socially produced, but dynamically changing, spaces that have histories and futures as well as present geographies connecting one space with another. We also recognize that spaces are not uniform; people with different cultural experiences and histories will experience the same place differently.

Classroom spaces are often very predictable, but school and classroom worlds can change. The teachers in this book create community learning spaces with young people over time as they arrange and rearrange physical and virtual environments in response to a group's energy and interests and particular students' needs; they institute predictable but responsive social practices like class meetings or field trips, make a wide range of literacy tools available for planned or novel negotiated activities in varied groupings, and access and create texts in print and online, as well as engage in ongoing actions and responses to particular students' desires and questions.

Creating Community Spaces for Learning

Literacy tools are especially instrumental at referencing, setting, and shaping the cultural norms, roles, beliefs, agendas, and purposes operating in a particular space that always has histories, and possible futures, as well being a meaningful present moment in which learning takes place. For example, at a ribbon cutting ceremony to celebrate a partnership between Indiana University and The Boys Academy in northwest Indiana, a district superintendent introduced the opening of the "Writers House" at the school with the following comments: "We envision the Writers House as a place where the students can develop their creative genius." Her remarks were soon given credence, as well as historical and cultural depth, by several of the sixth-grade student leaders who recited verse about their neighborhoods, families, and legacies inspired by George Ella Lyons's (1996) "Where I'm From," a poem made popular in schools by the teacher researcher and critical educator Linda Christensen (2000). One sixth-grader powerfully rendered the following work in a spoken-word format:

I am from loneliness and disparity
I am from a place where distance you cannot define
I've seen everything, heard everything, and been in everything

You hear me in the mist. Like a lizard changes its skin,
Hiding from everything in its surroundings

I am from a civilization that is from sea to shining sea
I descended from kings that came before me
Like Martin Luther King Jr., Malcolm X, Rosa Parks,
and many more that lived before me

I'm from my mom who means the world to me
The one that gave me life to be in this world and held me
Through the ups and downs
I am from the source of my tree, which will not end with me.
There will be a branch to take my spot,
but not just any branch, but a leader just like me.

I am from African Americans who fought for my freedom
in this country I call my homeland.
This is where I am from.

Teachers and students had decided that the literacy curriculum of the
Boys Academy would in part be driven by the following inquiry: "What is
our heritage and what will be our legacy?" This critical inquiry question
serves to shape the ongoing creation of a room dedicated to exploring and
sharing literacies. In a grassroots reform effort, the committed faculty at
the school, many themselves from the community, decided to refurbish an
old classroom into a Writers House, where the students could both create and go public with their literary, artistic, and creative forms of cultural
expression. The walls of the Writers House are now adorned with images
of famous African American authors. Books line the shelves, from canonical literature to more contemporary works of young adult fiction, graphic
novels, and biographies. There is a computer station for students' writing.
Set prominently in the center of the room is a stage, where the students
can perform, recite spoken-word poetry, rehearse powerful oratory, and use
words to connect with a range of audiences: family members, community
supporters, and outside visitors.

Spoken-word poetry became a shared centering tool and vehicle to
make a collaborative creative school space linked to family, neighborhood,
cultural experiences, and larger social issues. This is a social and cultural
learning space where both students and audience members can shape a community with meaning that transcends schooling's predominant emphasis on

individual achievement. Participating in the varied social literacy practices of composing, presenting, and interpreting, the students achieve agency in ways not always possible when curricula is driven by the testing paradigm. Additionally, students can adopt, and over time develop, identities as writers whose voices are honored for their effective and engaging use of a variety of literacy tools that include spoken-word poetry.

Experiencing and Studying Spaces

Administrators, teachers, parents, and other adults have the power to evaluate and the agency to control school spaces. How they share that power with one another, and with students, shapes the creation of space, how it is experienced, and thus what learning and teaching is possible. As illustrated by the Writers House, the ways in which school spaces are conceptualized in the shared imagination of adults and young people, and the literacy social practices that are supported, all make a difference regarding what actions, events, tools, emotions, and physical layouts are recognized and embraced as "appropriate" and thus what educational opportunities are made available.

Spaces are created and shaped across time through physical, social, verbal, and nonverbal interactions and activities focused on particular shared goals. Because space is experienced both collectively and differently, this reality can create social tensions when people have not agreed on broad purposes and particular acts. In contrast with the shared vision and agreed performances at the Boys Academy, the experience in most schools is quite different. For example, students who enter a classroom moving and talking about a recent event may encounter an adult who, expecting them to shift focus to a topic and an activity they have not agreed upon, encounters resistance when asking the young people to become still, be quiet, and read from a textbook that seems disconnected from their lives.

In classrooms where adults share power with young people by negotiating activities and goals, students can study how people outside, as well as inside school buildings, are continually using literacy tools to make and experience spaces by asking:

- Who has access to resources like pens, computers, television, or books?
- What social practices are shared?
- What activities are negotiable and with whom?
- How do people feel about what they are doing?
- How do people experience the space in similar/different ways?

"Thirdspace" theory (Soja, 1996) provides a way of understanding and critiquing how space is created and experienced and how it might be differently shaped. Firstspace is the physical, material, experienced aspect of space; it's how people perceive their being somewhere "here and now." Asking "How are you feeling right now about writing?" or "What so you think we should do now?" focuses attention on firstspace. Secondspace is what people conceive or are conceptualizing, often as "there and then." Asking, "What are you thinking about?" or "Where would you like to be?" focuses attention on secondspace.

Soja proposes that "thirdspace" embraces both first- and secondspaces that exist in a dynamic, inseparable "trialectic" relationship. When people seek out and create spaces that are both lived and conceptual, material and social, experiential and historical, real and imagined, then they create third-spaces. People giving answers to questions like, "Are you happy you are here?" or "How is what we are doing helping you to think?" indicate that they are in a thirdspace.

Thirdspaces emerge from tensions between false, inauthentic beliefs, narratives, and ideas—the notion that "deep down inside, we're all the same" or "anyone who just works hard can succeed in America"—and the felt realities of daily life captured in stories and images of differences in race, class, and gender or institutionalized economic inequalities. Teachers who embrace first- and secondspace contradictions and recognize their pedagogical opportunities can create thirdspaces in the classroom for inquiry focused on tensions between the social consequences of secondworld conceputalizations and firstspace lived realities, leading to creating thirdspace narratives of "counterstorytelling" (Vasudevan, 2006) that challenge dominant narratives.

Two Examples of Studying Spaces

In one critical inquiry project, high school students in a Los Angeles school district studied the disconnect between the rhetoric and the reality of students' right of equal access to public education. Early inquiries made them aware of a secondspace authority: according to the 14th Amendment, it is unconstitutional "for certain schools to provide a better education than others within the same state" (Morrell, 2008, p. 130). The students collected data related to test scores and dropout rates of California high schools indicating the firstspace reality of a wide disparity in the quality of these schools given their location: high-performing schools were located primarily in middle-class suburbs, with low-performing schools located primarily in low-income, high-minority areas. Their analysis led students to a conclusion that their potential to receive a high-quality high school education and be admitted to the University of California higher education system had largely to do with the area in which they happened to live.

The students used their analysis to critique a proposal from legislators that sought to abolish affirmative action programs related to admissions decisions based on race. Based on their study of the disparities in schools due to differences in race and class neighborhoods, the students noted that the proposed policy, which was ultimately rejected by the University of California Regents, would "have detrimental effects in California because activists and organizations like ACLU will no longer have statistics about the racial make-up of colleges and universities, and education inequalities will grow" (p. 131).

All of this led students to propose alternatives designed to change current education funding policies as well as ways to improve low-performing schools. Through participation in this critical inquiry project, students were learning to use literacy tools to interrogate schooling policies influencing their own lives.

In her own "third space" theory of literacy learning, Kris Gutiérrez (2008) describes ways in which students from nondominant communities have typically been subjected to deficit models of remedial education in schools that limit their sense of agency. In contrast, when these students participated in a rigorous summer project, the Migrant Student Leadership Institute (MSLI) at UCLA, they flourished and enhanced their sense of agency. Drawing on thirdspace theory, the program curriculum involved grappling with tensions between competing cultural and historical constructions of identities. In one activity, students drew on traditional *testimonio* oral sharing of life history with members of one's community to create written autobiographical narratives that portrayed tensions in border negotiations between their family's cultural worlds, often in Mexico, and their current cultural world of Los Angeles. In using the literacy tool of narratives, students became "designers of their own social futures. Part of this tool kit includes ways to understand better how to respond to oppression and to the consequences of poverty" (p. 156). The practices of designing and envisioning alternative futures were mediated in classroom discussions by the use of modals, metaphors, and uses of conditional ("what-if") language that invited students to entertain different possibilities for their future, as opposed to accepting deficit notions that they had no viable future.

Analyzing the Racialized, Gendered, and Classed Dimensions of Spaces

Young people can examine how different uses of language contribute to the creation of spaces and how they are differently interpreted. In particular, students could reflect on how spaces are conceptualized and perceived differently along lines of race, class, and gender.

Students' inquiries could consider how language and policies segregate spaces. In their analysis of Latino students' perceptions of segregated spaces within schools defined according to race, Barajas and Ronnkvist (2007) found that White spaces were created and reproduced through symbolic understandings of what it means to be "White" in a White space and what it means "not to be White" in a White space. Students in the school, particularly Latino/a students judged as less successful on standardized tests, uncovered experiences of their exclusion from what they perceived to be White spaces constituted by racialized school practices and policies, for example in relation to what language or dress is appropriate or how students are able to constitute and manage clubs.

Or they could study how different neighborhood spaces are described based on differences in race and/or class. In her history of the development of segregated neighborhoods since the 1920s, Sheryl Cashin (2004) notes that real estate policies and practices creating segregated neighborhoods served to drive up housing prices for homes assumed to be located in so-called desirable "White" neighborhoods. Such perceptions of neighborhoods, perpetuated by news broadcast portrayals of urban spaces that highlight crime, poverty, or behavior portrayed as problematic or deviant, are representations geared primarily for a suburban, middle-class audience who may then be critical of government support for urban spaces.

Students could conduct their own inquiry focused on how neighborhoods are portrayed as "desirable" or "undesirable" in the media and by realtors and local politicians. How are suburban upper-middle-class White areas with access to schools reporting high test scores represented as more "desirable" than poor, urban neighborhoods populated by people of color with low-performing schools? Students could also connect the discourses of national and local political rhetoric and action to inquire into how spaces have changed over time, for example looking at school segregation, desegregation, and resegregation in their own school district.

Or students could reflect on how spaces in stores are defined according to gender differences. For example, they may study how the signage and commercial images as well as the dress and language of employees in the "beauty" section of a department store that sells cosmetics or perfumes are collectively a discourse designed to create a primarily "feminine" space that at the same time is geared toward "selling products" to "adolescent" girls rather than educating them to be adult citizens.

Transformative Classroom Thirdspaces

Students often find that their actual lived experiences in and out of the classroom, their cultural resources, their home literacies, and their ideas about
social action are not considered significant for achieving academic objectives (Leander & Sheehy, 2004). In response, adults, like Gutiérrez, create
alternative-school thirdspaces for students.

Adults who are able to navigate secondspace constrictions and accept
firstspace realities can create lively classroom thirdspaces. Teachers who
collaboratively work with young people can harness students' energies,
past experiences, present abilities, and visions for the future. Active uses
of literacy tools in meaningful experiences will create classroom spaces
in which students can be aware of their potential as change agents; their
agency can transform lives when working with a teacher who builds on
their academic and social strengths, their cultural resources, and their
desires to help others.

Tracey Bigler-McCarthy spent a year transforming her classroom in an
alternative K–8 school, an ethnically and socioeconomically diverse lottery
school located in central Columbus, Ohio, into intercultural creative spaces
where children and adults collaborated to make art, raise money, and send
urgently needed materials to the Maulana School for 1,600 AIDS orphans
in Zimbabwe. The goal of her critical inquiry curriculum was to create an
alternative classroom space to help her K–1 students actively engage in imagining a different future for the African children and for themselves. The
work was focused by these questions: "How can we build community?"
and "How will our community include the people in the Maulana School?"
The students employed a range of literacy tools, that often involved active
collaboration with adults and older students: research the Shona culture;
compare lives in southern Africa with the children's lives in central Ohio;
send letters and drawings to Zimbabwe and reply to those sent in response;
learn to sculpt with a renowned Zimbabwean artist, Gedion Nyanhongo;
and interview the administrator of the charity they were helping. They also
planned a fund-raising exhibit for one Sunday afternoon at the local art
museum; they displayed and sold their paintings and sculptures depicting
visions of how people can connect across continents, as well as the artwork
of parents and local professional artists. The creation of a 16-panel mural
became a whole-school project that culminated in a dedication at a celebra-
tory dance attended by local politicians, artists, and educators. The mural
was then attached to a container that was shipped to Zimbabwe, filled with
books for children and young adults donated by The Ohio State University,

as well as clothes and educational and personal supplies gathered or purchased by the children and their parents.

In Tracey's transformed classroom space, students experienced agency rarely possible in schools; they fully participated in a transnational intercultural project that is making a difference in the lives of young people halfway round the world in a country almost entirely excluded from the global economy. These young people now know how literacy tools can be used to create and support lasting social change. As Tracey said in response to pictures of the container being opened in Zimbabwe,

> If we develop awareness, engage in meaningful dialogue and experiences which they and we care about, and negotiate a plan to work together as a community, children will realize and embrace the power to make change. When given this opportunity they easily access the set of tools needed to engage not only in social activism but also in any meaningful learning: caring and tenderness, questioning and reflection, exploration and sharing, and finally, culmination of the learning process through celebration.

ACTIVITIES FOR STUDYING SPACES

To study and represent how spaces are created, students could:

- Observe outside-school spaces using fieldnotes and collect media/visual representations (see also Chapter 9). Students could observe in fast food restaurants or in different shops at a mall, looking for which practices, roles, and language patterns are valued in different spaces, for example, how quickly people can order and receive food, how people are served differently, and how people speak to one another. They could interview customers about their perceptions in terms of what is or is not appealing to them about these spaces; expectations for desired practices, roles, and ways of talking; how they learned these expectations; and how they might like to change the space. They could compare and contrast with observations and interviews, for example in their own school lunchroom.
- Observe in school spaces. Observations can lead to inferential questions about the reason for consistent patterns in social practices: Do students segregate themselves by race in the

lunchroom because their friendships with peers occur in highly segregated neighborhoods? They could determine how students congregate with one another in parallel or overlapping spaces according to gender, race, and/or class differences, and then interview peers to determine their rationale for these groupings. Observational data in school could be compared with interview data and out-of-school observations.

- Identify tensions between firstspace realities and secondspace assumptions. Observations and interviews with authority figures and students could lead to a critique of the ways in which spaces are hierarchically constructed and represented through different competing discourses of, for example, schooling, race, class, and gender.
- Formulate more complex thirdspace representations by synthesizing the tensions between firstspace experiences and secondspace perceptions or representations of spaces. For example, students could create thirdspace alternative representations and stories about their school that acknowledge differences and divisions but celebrate diversity to present a vision of hoped-for transformation.

THREE

How Do We Use Literacy Tools to Enact Identities and Establish Agency?

Dominator culture has tried to keep us all afraid, to make us choose safety instead of risk, sameness instead of diversity. Moving through that fear, finding out what connects us, reveling in our differences, this is the process that brings us closer, that gives us a world of shared values, of meaningful community.
—bell hooks, *Teaching Community*, p. 197

In this chapter, we describe examples of students enacting identities and establishing agency through productively and collaboratively taking risks, and on occasions confronting fears, to take ethical action that made differences in their communities inside and outside school. In collaboration with peers and supportive adults, students use literacy tools to enact identities that establish their sense of agency: They begin to recognize that they can change both themselves and the world. Over time they may, for example, become known as a "captivating storyteller," a "bookworm," an "inquiring mind," a "dramatic guy," a "talented writer," a "creative artist," or a "computer whiz." They may also become known as "people who make a difference."

USING LITERACY TOOLS TO ENACT IDENTITIES

In using literacy tools to enact identities in supportive environments, young people can construct themselves as having agency—possessing the ability, confidence, and expertise to bring about change. For example, as a student in Melissa's Writing as Performance, Art, and Communications class at North High School, Minneapolis, in 2001, Donnie formulated and asked herself critical inquiry questions such as, "Who am I going to be?" and "How can I reveal my identity as a strong Black woman?" She used these questions as tools to reflect on her identity as well as challenge the paucity of positive images of Black adolescent females in dominator culture. In an interview with Melissa 7 years later she noted that, "In high school, there were no images in the media [of Black females] that looked like me. I had this story I decided I was going to be who I wanted to be." Focused on the critical inquiry questions grounding the coursework that term, "How are strengths born from experience?" and "How is identity conveyed through our art forms?," Donnie began to use another literacy tool, spoken-word poetry. She reflected on her creative process, drawing on experiences in her church and the rich body of African American poets and performers she was exposed to:

> Growing up, I did recitations at my AME [African Methodist Episcopal] church during Black History month of famous African American people, like Sojourner Truth; I was never afraid of the stage. During high school, KMOJ [the local community radio station] played Black female artists like India Arie, Lauryn Hill, and Erykah Badu.

Donnie recalled how these artists inspired her sense of self and her uses of writing to construct an identity beyond ascriptions of victimhood. She used spoken-word poetry as one tool to enact an identity that resisted the perceived labels and expectations put on her by society. In her poem "Nappy Roots," written when she was a high school student, Donnie began to construct a positive identity based on images of natural beauty and "okayness" associated with being a Black female.

Nappy Roots

My edges were straight
But I had nappy roots.
American Culture
Devours individuality
Like vultures on prey.
Making you believe
Your physical appearance
Isn't okay
So like
If I don't like
Have like
Long, silky straight hair
Then that makes me like
Not pretty, like right?
I can perm my hair

And perm my hair
But every six weeks
Reality grows there
And the dark came to the light
When the naps returned . . .
When I needed a touch up . . .
But it was actually a touch down
And my self-esteem was the underdog . . .
And that game was lost . . .
Torturing my head was imitation
And imitation was my initiation
Into being accepted.
My edges were straight
But I was on the edge of insanity
Being someone that wasn't me.
I was on the edge of a cliff
And if European beauty jumped
Maybe, just maybe, I would have jumped
Too.

I've got black woman lips
Black woman hips
And sun-kissed skin.
Not to mention a black woman attitude.
I left the B.S. institute
And started to home school.
My edges were straight
But I had nappy roots.
No matter how tall the tree
It always has roots
And without roots
The tree dies
And I was on the route
To self-hate
And my tree wasn't bearing any fruit.
If you plant apples you don't get oranges
So where did I get the crazy idea
That nappy was not right?
            Can't go no where
            Cause hair ain't combed

Can't let nobody see me like this
See me at my essence
Vulnerable and pure
Confident and true
Rather have chemically damaged hair
Than outkastic nappy hair
By American standards
My hair is all the way bad
It's dreadlocked
And I dread the fact that
Some people don't love themselves enough
To be natural
I dread the fact that
Some people have to be filled with artificial
Flavors
To taste good
I dread the fact
That my people don't love themselves.
I'm locked within my reality
And on the edge of myself.
I dread jumping into your mentality
My edges are nappy
And I've now got nappy roots
I am beautiful because beauty is
Truth

In this poem, Donnie describes how her "nappy roots" mark her identity as someone who deviates from dominant and distorted media images of Eurocentric beauty. Though this leads her to initially doubt her own self-worth, she also realizes that one's worth involves more than appearance and that she doesn't need to conform to external expectations. She can embrace herself as she is. As she enacts an identity as someone who resists conformity to mass media images, she also has agency to challenge these socially constructed norms about female beauty that she began to recognize as artificial.

Donnie is thus engaged in quite sophisticated intellectual critique. She is not merely subscribing to a more expansive and inclusive notion of physical beauty. She is also challenging the very idea of a model of physical beauty itself in and of itself, which in any iteration will involve some form of exclusion. Her poem suggests that beauty has more to do with truth, and truth is found not in surfaces but in deeply rooted personal and collective histories and legacies. The epistemic privilege of Donnie's social location enables her to have profound insights with respect to universal human worth.

Donnie's poem reveals that identity is not fixed, but shifts as she moves across different worlds. People may enact different possible identities by trying out novel uses of languages, narratives, or images to shape or transform social relationships in particular spaces. Through improvising their uses of literacy tools and over time reflecting on the meaning and implications of them, students can socially construct what Holland, Lachicotte, Skinner, and Cain (1998) refer to as *narrative* identities: "people tell others who they are, but even more important they tell themselves and then try to act as though they are who they say they are" (p. 3). Donnie is using her poem as a tool for telling herself, and others, new stories about who she is and how she can act: She acquires agency as a beautiful young Black woman who can resist oppressive mainstream American norms of hairstyle and beauty.

People's identities are also affected by, and enacted through, how they position others and others position them in daily interactions. Judith Butler (1990, 1993) stresses the "performativity" of life and how subjectivities (or subject positions), like one's gender or one's identity as a student, are socially constructed over time through interactions that "normalize" how different types of people ought to behave. Teachers spend a great deal of time trying to "socialize" young people into particular types of "students" by channeling their agency in "appropriate" ways that too often can erase or diminish their social, ethnic, or cultural identities. Butler has additionally shown how people, including women like Donnie who are negatively positioned by others, can actively resist such subject positions and in response shape their identities. They can begin to do so, for example, by raising questions about implicit cultural norms in mass media images and enacting agency in poetry as part of a move toward social change. Donnie's poem also demonstrates how identity is not merely formed in the negative, in response to the oppression of socially sanctioned norms. It also has an integrity of its own, serving as a source of collective joy, strength, and wisdom.

In enacting identities, people position others. As adults enact their identity as teachers, they can position young people in positive or deficit ways that affect their sense of agency. Teachers' deficit positioning of students as incapable or incompetent, for example, can push young people into both accepting negative views of themselves and developing an oppositional identity of resistance and rejection. In contrast, teachers may position students as competent and capable and cultivate the humility to learn from them. They do so by creating classroom spaces that support students' uses of literacy tools for positive enactments of identities (Biesta & Tedder, 2007). For example, teachers may encourage students to engage in "code meshing" (Young, 2007, p. 7) to combine African American Vernacular English, White English, and Pinoy (Filipino English) vernacular codes, to challenge essentialist categorizations of both language and identity.

Teachers also affect student agency when they create spaces for students' competent performances of the use of various literacy tools. When young people create, present, and/or watch each other's performances, they are engaged in key literacy social practices of composing, making public, and interpreting texts. Yet at the same time they are both using and developing their identities.

Stage performances, spoken-word poetry, reading aloud, and speaking as characters from a story (and other ways of using dramatic inquiry as described in Chapter 5) are all examples of dramatic performances in the sense that people are, for a few moments or an extended period of time, dramatizing an improvised aspect of life in an imagined space. How dramatic improvisation is regarded and supported in classrooms makes a difference for how young people take up alternative ways of being in the world that they explore and enact to shape or develop their everyday life identities. Donnie, for example, imagined and performed herself as a very different person from the way she had been positioned and understood in most of her schooling.

Dramatic performances contrast with nondramatic performances, such as sharing ideas in a discussion or the everyday enactment of social roles or subjectivities. Because nondramatic performances are in everyday rather than playful aesthetic spaces, they tend to be less improvised, so that young people have fewer possibilities for collaboratively exploring different ways of identifying with other people and acting in the world.

USING LITERACY TOOLS TO EXPLORE AND QUESTION IDENTITIES

In contrast with Donnie's positive self-affirming identity, some students may have a sense of agency in relation to an identification that teachers may want to question because of its antisocial assumptions and implications, for example, in relation to an issue like bullying. However, direct critique can be difficult if students perceive this as a social or cultural challenge, especially when schooling promotes a very fragmented community. Dramatic improvisation can create imagined spaces in which cultural assumptions can be questioned when teachers collaboratively assist young people to explore previously unconsidered identifications so that they may reconsider their agency.

Mary Ann Buchan was a student teacher in 2009 in a 7th-grade classroom at a large ethnically and socioeconomically diverse urban school in Columbus, Ohio, with over 3,500 discipline actions annually, of which a large percentage were for bullying, though not in her classroom. One student wrote anonymously in a survey that revealed that 25% of students in the classroom engaged in bullying behavior: "Bullying is everywhere at home and school and it's at our school too. Lots of people fight and bother people, but don't talk about it." Mary Ann wanted the students to consider ways they could act as allies to victims of bullying as part of a nonviolent conflict resolution approach.

Over her 5-week placement period, by reading the young adult novel *The Revealers* by Doug Wilhelm (2005) (http://www.the-revealers.com), which has bullying as its theme, Mary Ann wanted to explore this central topic. At the heart of the novel is the agency of three victims of emotional and physical torment who create and organize the "Revealer" school Web site, which acts as a hotline for reports of bullying. It is here that kids have a voice, share their stories, and reveal in public the bullying behavior of people that includes girls, boys, and affluent and impoverished students.

In initial oral and written responses to the novel, many students made it clear that they did not identify much with the victims of bullying nor with the characters attempting to be allies. Rather, about three-quarters said they most related to the male character who bullies through fighting, many inferring that the character had an abusive father. Further, many blamed the victims, describing them as "nerds" or "lames." A major question the students agreed to ask the author during a video conference planned for weeks later was, "Why don't the victims fight back?" The response of one young person was representative of the dominant reaction of all the students. Mary Ann noted that

> Desiree was a very headstrong, confident, and popular girl. In response to the haughty White character, Bethany, who passed verbally aggressive notes to bully Catalina, a Filipina newcomer to the school, Desiree said she felt sorry for Catalina, recognized she wouldn't stand up for herself, and believed that Bethany needed to be taught a lesson. She said she would have gathered a few of her friends together to beat up Bethany and stop the verbal attacks. In class discussions her classmates took similar positions: The dominant classroom discourse assumed that reactive violence was the best response to stop harassment.

Knowing that dramatic improvisation creates spaces in which students can try out different identifications, Mary Ann strategically engaged students in various dramatic activities over the following weeks. These focused on the following critical inquiry questions: Why do people bully, how do they use power, what are the consequences of bullying, and what are effective responses?

- The students wrote monologues as if they were characters, initially from the viewpoint of a character "like yourself" and then from the position of a character "unlike yourself."
- Small groups dramatized a verse from the lyrics of the popular culture song "Hero" by Superchick that advocates supporting victims of bullying and other social problems, as if they were in the situations described by the narrators. They were then interviewed by classmates taking on the role of reporters; subsequently, the whole class watched and discussed the interviews, which had been videotaped.
- Mary Ann took on the role of the privileged, manipulative, and defensive bullying girl, Bethany, in an invented scene that drew on other exchanges in the novel with the protagonist, Russell. As they are working on an assignment together, he asks why she is bullying Catalina. He was represented in turn initially by those students who were most eager to take on those roles—and then by others who had been reticent to do so.
- In a whole-group improvisation, students took on various roles in another invented scene: Bethany's powerful lawyer father attempts to pressure the principal into censoring and closing down the Revealer Web site that covers stories of his daughter's bullying and lying behavior.
- Students wrote individual letters as if to the Revealer Web site.
- In ongoing discussions, students considered who had the most power in situations as well as how effective characters were in resisting other people and using what power they had.

Adopting change-based assessment, Mary Ann evaluated the effectiveness of using dramatic improvisation. She noted that in contrast with their initial disengaged attitude, "Once we talked together as if we were characters the students began to enthusiastically read and interpret the novel and they gained deep levels of understanding from the viewpoints of all the major characters. Additionally, the students took on a newfound sense of competence and success." She also noted that "several students who were used to being powerful in their everyday lives said they experienced the frustrations of having little power. One boy who often ran foul of the school authorities expressed his frustration about not having his power respected."

Many students who had previously only minimally identified with victims wrote to the fictional Revealer Web site to tell tales of bullying. Desiree was one of those who wrote empathetically in the voice of Catalina, the Filipina newcomer.

> Why do the mean girls think they need to make fun of me all the time? They don't know me. All I want to do is go home to the Philippines 'cause I miss my mom. That Bethany thinks she is so much better than me. Why does she need to treat me wrong just to make herself look good? I'm a person too, just like them. I don't deserve this.

On the last day of the unit the students participated in a live video conference with author Doug Wilhelm, who spoke from Vermont. Students were no longer so dismissive about the actions of the bullying victims; they asked the author questions that focused on his inspiration for the book, his own previous experiences of bullying, and if he had plans for a sequel. In an e-mail afterward, Wilhelm wrote, "It was obvious that your students had thoroughly read and contemplated *The Revealers*. Their insightful questions and attentive behavior during the videoconference was exemplary, and please have them email me with any further questions they may have about the story" (Wilhelm, e-mail correspondence, May 5, 2009).

In a concluding discussion about how they might respond to bullying, several students said they now saw the importance of courageously standing up for yourself; many others thought that reaching out as an ally or a friend would make a big difference to someone being bullied. One of Desiree's comments suggested a shift in her school social identity and her agency as a potential ally in relation to oppressive behavior. Speaking about a girl in the school who was frequently harassed, she said, "There's a girl I feel sorry for her 'cause she gets picked on and they egg her on. I'm trying to be nice to her and I actually talked with her for five minutes. Maybe if I'm her friend she might not need protection." As Mary Ann noted at the end of her placement period, "Though some of her peers gasped when she said that, as a leader in the group hopefully she will be an influential example to other students in the future."

IMPLICATIONS FOR ENACTING IDENTITIES

All that we have written about suggests that the identities students construct are affected by the spaces teachers create and the literacy tools teachers access and make available for use with students:

- Students can experiment with and shape identities through dramatic performance, writing, or other forms of dramatic improvisation, for example, through spoken-word poetry, taking on the role of literary characters, and (as we discuss further in Chapters 5 and 7) assuming the roles of experts or consultants.
- Students have more agency in relation to their identity formation when using literacy tools if they reflect with supportive but challenging adults about the possible consequences and implications for individuals and communities of different identifications.
- Digital literacy tools significantly extend the ways in which students interact and thus identify with peers and with people from multiple networks around the world.

CONSTRUCTING AGENCY THROUGH
LITERACY TOOLS

Agency is interrelated with how people enact their identities. We define agency as having the potential or capacity to enact change in status-quo practices, beliefs, or self-perceptions. As Biesta and Tedder (2007) note: "Agency, in other words, is not something that people have; it is something that people do. This concept of agency highlights that actors always act by means of an environment rather than simply in an environment" (p. 136).

People's agency affects their identity and vice versa. Students who view themselves as change agents believe that they can make a difference in the world. They are willing not only to voice their beliefs about the need for change but also to enact change through active participation despite difficulties. And when they understand how they have acted, or could act, as others have to make a difference, they change their understandings of who they are and might become. Thus, adults need to plan activities and shape environments that allow students to have agency as they use literacy tools to record and discuss how others have changed the world and how they might envision and make differences in their own lives inside and outside the classroom.

Agency and Voice

One basic literacy tool that engages others in communication, promotes social change, and shapes identities is that of voice—the use of language in particular spaces to project a persona and stance along with particular values and beliefs.

Students are often inspired to enact agency by drawing on the voices of other change agents they admire—the words of public figures such as Martin Luther King, Sojourner Truth, Robert Kennedy, Malcolm X, Gloria Steinman, and Barack Obama as well as those of other revered people like grandparents, family friends, or fictional characters from enduring narratives. Students make these voices their own by listening to and using them, along with their attendant beliefs, discourses, frameworks, and partcipating in what Bakhtin (1981) has described as "double-voicing."

Trying out new voices is not enough. Essential to assuming agency is the extent to which students have the opportunity or potential to propose and make actual change both within and outside the classroom. Simply engaging in "knowing-telling," regurgitation activities that reify existing knowledge, affords them little opportunity to adopt alternative voices associated with the sort of "epistemic agency" grounded in particular ways of framing the world, which are needed to sustain acts of change (Scardamalia, 2002). For example, in reflecting on discrimination in schooling, a student may echo Malcolm X's belief in the need for African Americans to challenge institutional racism, or a student may draw on the words of the prophet Mohammed to promote tolerance in response to religious hate speech in the news or in a novel. And in dramatic activities, students' agency is shaped by whatever ethical, legal, scientific, religious, economic, or technological voices they assume as they enact roles and improvise with the related identities constituted by these discourses.

One key aspect of agency is awareness that one has the ability or possibility to make change by using alternative voices to those of the mainstream. The playfulness and performativity of dramatic spaces promote such awareness. Theater performances and the sort of dramatic improvisation described above, as well as the dramatic inquiry we discuss in Chapter 5, are all powerful literacy tools for assisting young people to shape and use voices to intentionally explore issues and enact change in imagined spaces that may affect agency in everyday life.

A formal theater production example comes from Jan Mandell's Intermediate Acting class at a St. Paul high school, where the students collaboratively wrote and performed an original play about the democratic process during the 2008 election. The 30-minute production, *Your One Vote,* addressed the questions "How will our lives be affected by candidates' choices?" and "Will the voices of young people be heard?" Ashley, a 16-year-old student actor in the class, wrote a piece entitled "Equality" that included these lines: "I'll fight for you, I'll fight for me, we'll make a change, equality." In an interview she spoke of her uncertainty in not knowing her own voice or thoughts on political issues, as she tended to "go along with the crowd." In contrast, she stressed that in the basement-black-box-theater space, "Down here is the only place I can really be me." Iris, another 16-year-old student actor, created a voice to speak for those whose voices were not audible to many in society. Speaking of her performance piece, "Stand for Me," she explained: "I wrote about people without a voice. . . . I wanted to show voices from the past, present and future: an unborn baby, a man on parole, a person who has passed away, a fifteen-year-old."

Agency and Recognizing Change in the Status Quo

When students recognize that their actions can change the status quo, they may have more confidence in their abilities as change agents. Linda Flower (2008) describes how a group of young people living in a Pittsburgh neighborhood worked together with other residents to challenge an attempt by the Pittsburgh police to impose a curfew on their neighborhood as a means of reducing crime. These young people dialogically responded to the issue as they wrote pamphlets and distributed them to neighbors and law enforcement to argue their position that curfews, as indicated by research, are not effective in curbing crime and may actually only further exacerbate the problem. Their protests led to a neighborhood meeting of all the affected parties, where having heard from the young people and engaging in dialogue with them, law enforcement dropped their plan to impose a curfew. Flower attributes the young people's success to their sense of agency, defined as thoughtful, engaged, collaborative enactment and reflection on what is worthy or significant:

> This collaboration involves dialogic interaction that values the agency of others, particularly marginalized others who are assumed to lack agency according to elite standards. Students acquire this dialogic agency through collectively responding to others' acts and voices, in terms of their willingness to go public, to engage in a dialogue that listens, speaks, and expects a response to which they are prepared to respond. (Flower, 2008, p. 205)

Because the Pittsburgh students' actions led to ending the curfew, on reflection they were able to recognize that, against overwhelming odds, they could achieve change. These students realized the value of strength in numbers by mobilizing members of their neighborhood to challenge the curfew.

In other situations small groups of young people with access to digital literacy tools, like camera cell phones and Twitter, have effectively mobilized large protests (Shirky, 2009). At the time of writing (June 2009), the huge demonstrations in Iran articulating voices of protest, largely organized, broadcast to the world, and interpreted via young people's digital communications, powerfully illustrates the potential sociopolitical power of combining digital with other literacy tools.

While students sometimes lack the power or authority to make lasting changes in their schools, they may still experience a sense of agency by sensing their potential to propose and publicly imagine change. Students are most likely to recognize their ability to make change through planning and organizing events, but they may also do so through discussions, journal/blog writing, Internet surfing, or artwork, especially when related to events in their daily lives. And in related dramatic improvisation, students may share and perform their experiences and hopes with peers and adults, leading both groups to perceive how others can and do achieve change and how they might also do so.

FOSTERING USE OF LITERACY TOOLS TO ACHIEVE AGENCY

Students' uses of literacy tools are most likely to help them achieve agency if they can do the following:

- Draw on the voices and the related social and ethical frameworks associated with those of people they admire.
- Apply their experiences of agency from other contexts in which they have expertise or status, for example, drawing on their virtual or digital experiences in actual or imagined communities that include literary and virtual game worlds.
- Work through collective action to pool their ideas, resources, and expertise to achieve change.
- Recognize, share, and value how their own and others' successes in achieving change enhances their sense of agency.

We argue that for students to be able to use the tools of global communication networks, and pragmatically to be more successful in a knowledge-based economy, teachers need to support and extend students' learning to combine digital and other literacy tools. The 21st century heralds classroom spaces where young people and adults can collaboratively use diverse literacy tools to embrace differences, shape identities, and extend agency, creating communities and worlds that are more open and ready to embrace and learn from young people's energy and ideas.

FOUR

Narrative

Surfacing Buried Histories

A person who is insensitive to the suffering of his fellows is that way because he lacks the imaginative power to get under the skin of another human being and see the world through eyes other than his own.

—Chinua Achebe, *Hopes and Impediments*, p. 98

One of the most productive exercises in Gerald's teacher education courses involves inviting his university students to read and think about how they would respond to the personal experience narratives of elementary-age children from immigrant, migrant, and refugee backgrounds. In considering these pieces, the university students are asked to describe the strengths of the writer, imagine what else they might want to know about the author, and consider the role of the writer's knowledge in orchestrating the elementary language arts curriculum. One of the writing samples that Gerald usually shares is an initial draft of a vignette written by a 10-year-old fifth grader, Kendal, entitled "Multicultural Neighborhood":

> If I was somebody's next door neighbor, I would teach them how to speak my native language Visayan, and they would teach me their language too. If the neighbors have just migrated, I would show them around the block of our street. Then I will teach them at school to learn English and make them very proud.
>
> If my neighbors say to take drugs or tobacco, I will say "no" because it could make you die or get sick. Hopefully they would agree that they shouldn't take drugs. The other way to help my next door neighbor is to grow crops in the backyard and donate the surplus to them.
>
> How to teach my neighbors? I would take them to school to be smarter. Then I would teach them what their homework is and play with them when they are accomplished with their work. We might play basketball or play hide-and-go seek.

If my neighbor is alongside of a brook, I will go to them and teach
them how to fish. I love to teach people from other cultures, even if
they are different than me.

The university students who have worked with this piece have responded
to it in a number of different ways, even within the same assignment. One
not uncommon impulse involves honing in on what the essay needs or lacks:
for example, a better approximation of conventions, a further elaboration
of details, or a more linear structure. Many of the university students have
either an implicit or explicit idea of what an essay or narrative should
entail—often learned throughout their own processes of schooling—and
are understandably concerned that Kendal learn academic conventions, the
power codes, for which he may soon be evaluated. This type of response,
although reasonable and well-meaning, sometimes turns out to have more
to do with the future teachers' assumptions about students' identities and
capabilities, the role of the teacher, and of academic writing and literacy
than with insights into the actual piece itself.

University students have also adopted a different stance toward the
work: Instead of viewing the piece as deviating from a preconceived ideal,
they begin with the assumption that students are emerging poets and artists
who are engaged in the process of communicating something that matters,
that may have at once profound personal and collective significance. This
stance often involves a suspension of judgment and a genuine curiosity and
willingness to learn from and with the students. In the spirit of the work of
Patricia Carini and the Prospect School (2001), the emphasis is placed not
on a generic model of the ideal student or ideal work, but rather on "the
power of the particular" to articulate evolving values, identities, and ethos
that also have shared and general relevance.

Adopting an inquiry stance, this type of response will often entail describing what is present in the work and then asking further questions to
get a sense of the intentions of the author. The university students might
suggest inviting the child to tell them more about the language of Visayan,
what his life was like back in the Philippines, and how he has negotiated the
crossing of cultural boundaries. They may want to know how the child has
come, at such a young age, to care so deeply for the needs and well-being
of others. Some of the university students have decided that the best way to
honor the student's story would be by sharing some of their own. Perhaps
they are migrants themselves or have spent time helping others. If the future
teachers were to reciprocate in kind, with their own "histories connected
to experience" (Morrison, 1994), there may be a fundamentally different
potential for collaborative creation. The opening up of the teacher might

inspire other stories by other students. Through the sharing and braiding of experience, both teachers and students could enter into a "community of meaning" (Sánchez-Casal & Macdonald, 2002), where narrative becomes a means of fortifying relational bonds as well a vehicle for engaging ever deeper levels of inquiry.

NARRATIVE AS A LITERACY TOOL

Personal narratives are the stories people tell to make sense of their experiences. Across disciplines—including psychology, folklore, anthropology, historiography, and literary theory—there has been a near-consensus that the function of narrative is not merely to transparently record and depict reality "as it is," in some unmediated or pristine state. It is, rather, one of the primary tools by which agents interpret and constitute the world, what Jerome Bruner (1996) has famously labeled the "narrative construal of reality." The anthropologist Renato Rosaldo (1993) suggests that stories "contribute to the reality of their participants" and play a role in "making" events and history (p. 129). This emphasis on "making" draws attention to issues of power and privilege and the procreative role that language plays in constructing the world. It raises questions such as the following: Whose stories matter? Whose stories are obscured? What does it mean to have contesting narrative understandings of an experience, event, or history? Who creates the stories we accept as truth? If our understandings of ourselves, others, and the world are invariably mediated by narrative, do certain stories distort our abilities to "read the world" accurately? Conversely, are there better, more enabling stories that portray a truer sense of personal or collective identity? Are there stories that provide us with more complete explanations of the world we share or orient our actions to a clearer vision of the world we might want to share?

The Nigerian postcolonial writer Chinua Achebe (1988) famously articulated the relationship between narrative and power in his thunderous critique of Conrad's *Heart of Darkness*. Achebe ultimately concludes that the novel is racist because it misrepresents the African people as a homogeneous background mass whose sole purpose is to serve as a "prop" or "foil" for the spiritual development or deterioration of the European characters. One of the mechanisms by which Conrad dehumanizes the Africans is by objectifying them as "limbs or rolling eyes" (p. 6). But even more telling, the Africans are forbidden the ability to speak; their language is reduced to, quoting Conrad himself, a " 'violent babble of uncouth sounds" or "'grunting phrases'" (pp. 8–9). While the eloquent fictional narrative provides penetrating insight into its European protagonists' psyches, the Africans themselves are denied their own narratives and, by implication, a history and a humanity. Their stories are not taken seriously; they are not even heard. Conrad, of course, was a brilliant writer of his own time and place who provoked European colonists to look at themselves in the mirror. Nevertheless, Achebe speaks to the need of having multiple perspectives in any literary or literacy curriculum.

THE POWER OF NARRATIVE

What does it mean to take students' stories seriously in educational contexts? One rationale for inviting students to share their stories is to better understand how they can use their background knowledge to gain access to curricular content. Stories also have an obvious interpersonal value because they enable students to weave their unique histories into the fabric of the classroom community. Nevertheless, for the most part, educators still think of stories as a lower-grade cognitive phenomenon not necessarily conducive to higher-level thinking and, at best, as a starting place for more serious academic work.

Student narratives are far more significant than that. We believe that providing safe spaces for students to share stories is a fundamental requirement for a democratic education and a generative condition for intellectual and ethical investigation. The ability to narrativize is a universal human capacity. But what narratives mean and the social practices through which they are enacted vary across cultures, local contexts, and genres. The Native American literary critic Sean Kicummah Teuton (2008) provides a powerful example of this variance. The American *bildungsroman* (or coming-of-age tale) often tells the story of a young person seeking fortune in a foreign land, and both reinforces and promotes ideologies of individual transformation and upward mobility. In contrast, Teuton notes that those written by Native American people during the Red Power movement "exude a yearning to return to the homeland from which the protagonist has become estranged" (p. 36). In these works, personal growth is inextricably and intimately connected to the growth of the community. The pedagogical value of multiple stories is not simply that different groups have different stories, but, more importantly, that particular stories have universal significance. Narratives are therefore vehicles for linking subjective experience to more complete knowledge about our shared world, especially for individuals who speak or write from buried or misrepresented histories or who don't hear the echo of their own experiences in the traditional school curriculum.

Kendal's piece, which we shared at the beginning of this chapter, embodied an alternative value system that contrasted with the school's focus on individual performance; it has continued to take on a life of its own as a vehicle for university students to think about the ways in which culture inflects writing. It may be important to reiterate that we are sharing an early written draft because we are interested in thinking about how we might learn from, respond to, and support student work through an inquiry and change-based assessment paradigm. The first thing we might notice is that Kendal seems to be posing his own *inquiry* by structuring his narrative around a hypothetical situation: "If" he had a neighbor who was a newcomer or had just migrated, how would he interact with them? Kendal's piece illustrates "the interrelated evaluative and social functions" of stories (Dyson & Genishi, 1998, p. 2). He becomes a "commentator on significant life experiences" that have immediate pertinence to his community.

There are a few contextual factors to Kendal's inquiry that are worth noting. Kendal is writing his story from his own social location as a migrant. His family had recently arrived in the area in search of economic and political stability. His piece was also written at a time when there was a resurgence of nativism in the area, which was manifesting itself in English-only sentiments and calls to close the border. We can therefore see in Kendal's words the seeds of what Critical Race Theorists (Bonilla-Silva, 2001) call a "counternarrative" to dominant discourses surrounding migrants and immigration. Kendal imagines his community as a *space* where newcomers are welcomed, even embraced. He also asserts the value of multiliteracy. He promises to teach his neighbors both English and his family language of Visayan. The newcomers have their own language that they would teach him, as part of what the Filipino poet and novelist Carlos Bulosan (2005) calls a process of "mutual speech." Also implied in this sharing is mutual edification. The characteristics of Kendal's imagined space challenge the restorative nostalgia of those who would long for a homogenous neighborhood.

Taking Kendal's narrative seriously, therefore, entails understanding the ways in which it articulates an emerging, if inchoate, political and ethical vision. Politically, Kendal's piece prefigures a neighborhood ethos of pluralism rather than one of assimilation. He is finding a way to connect his particular identity as someone with Filipino ancestors with the experiences of others. In the process of shared and overlapping experience, there is the potential for Kendal to develop a sense of solidarity with other immigrants in the community. Kendal is deeply concerned that his neighbors have access to basic needs and rights, including food and a quality education. Many of the elementary students in Gerald's class did in fact achieve *agency* by participating in a neighborhood social action movement to advocate for universal health care, including for undocumented families and children. Some protested the dismantling of bilingual education. And a number, as they grew older, became active youth leaders in the immigrant rights movement. In part, these projects were nurtured by the sharing of autobiographical narratives like Kendal's.

The students' commitments and desires for change were not an abstract political platform. They grew out of knowledge embedded in the first-space immediacy and rawness of their experiential worlds, from which they derived insight into both human vulnerability and potential. Kendal's narrative expresses a "felt need" to create a community that is close to the land, where the most vulnerable are cared for and neighbors enjoy one another. We believe this emerging ethical vision emphasizes a sense of collective well-being in which the health of a community is only as robust as its most vulnerable members. Conversely, the devaluing or exclusion of any individual compromises everyone's cognitive and ethical growth. Students' narratives can become an opening to inquiry into structural inequality and toward societal space not predicated on individual competition and advancement but on collective flourishing. Their works "embody alternative anti-hegemonic accounts of what is significant and in fact necessary for a more accurate understanding of the world" (Mohanty, 1997, pp. 237–238).

Attentive to the disparity between deficit perspectives of immigrant students and their ethical, political, and intellectual capaciousness as evidenced in their narratives, Gerald asked his fifth graders to make a list of all that they did to take care of their families and communities. Students then selected particular items on which to elaborate. Kendal identified the following responsibilities:

I help my mom wash the dishes.
I help my brother babysit.
I help fold the laundry.
I help cook rice.
I help my family clean the house.
I help my mom water the plant.
I help my mom clean the yard.
I help fix my cousin's tree house.
I help my mom cut the tree.
I help my brother wash the car.
I help cut the grass.
I help cook eggs and hot dogs.
I help send clothes to the Philippines.
I help my relatives build the house.

Kendal's list, like his neighborhood narrative, is not merely a set of stories that contribute to the plurality of the classroom community. Rather, these writings articulate a different set of values—an alternative view of the world that can shape the learning of the classroom community. Kendal describes caring for people, locally and transnationally, through helping with chores, watching and feeding siblings, sending material goods to support distant relatives, and participating in communal constructions of shelter. These commitments embody *bayanihan* work—the spirit of cooperation that has its roots in the Filipina/o tradition of gathering together to help relocate a member of the community by physically carrying their house to a new site. Kendal's narratives—his hopes for his community, his list of daily acts of love and labor—contribute to opportunities for reenvisioning the culture of the classroom. Rather than assimilating Kendal, and all the students, into a predetermined school ideology where individual worth is measured by deviations from a norm, the communal orientation of many student narratives can help us imagine a classroom where all members are supporting one another. Kendal's work is not just one of a range of perspectives that merely coexists in school; it is also potentially a guiding ideal. Gerald's students did in fact work to create a communitarian space where learning was collaborative, where one person's success was everyone's success and one person's struggle was everyone's struggle.

The lists composed by other students in the class named a range of experiences and responsibilities: getting siblings ready for school, acting as cultural and linguistic mediators for their families, helping their parents clean houses, living in refugee camps, and longing for parents who work in Alaskan canneries. One of Kendal's classmates used her initial list to write a narrative that poignantly described picking asparagus with her grandmother, noting the blazing sun, the stoop labor, the dirt under the fingernails, and the disbelief and pride that an elderly woman could last 8 hours when she could only last 15 minutes. As Achebe (1988) argues, narratives can help us understand the world in "other people's skins" (p. 101). The writings of Kendal and his peers provided an opportunity for the classroom community to learn from one another's experiences and expand their epistemic horizons.

RECOMMENDATIONS FOR
VALUING NARRATIVE

How, then, can we honor students' stories and experiences? Because teaching is about the creative alchemy and open-ended potential of a particular community of learners, there is no easy blueprint to follow. Instead, we suggest several approaches that can help educators develop a stance that supports and builds on students' narratives.

Teach Books That Represent a Multiplicity of Experiences

Books can validate students' experiences and provide teachers with models and a springboard from which to solicit students' own narratives. There are a number of examples relevant to diverse classrooms, including Francisco Jimenez's (1999) autobiographical novella *The Circuit* and the picture book *My Diary from Here to There; Mi Diario de aquí hasta allá*, written by Amanda Irma Perez (2002) and illustrated by Maya Christina Gonzalez. Even for younger students, teachers may carefully select passages from adult novels, such as Carlos Bulosan's (1974) *America Is in the Heart* or Esmeralda Santiago's (2006) *When I Was Puerto Rican*, both of which address experiences and histories excluded from the standardized curriculum.

Allow Students to Make Canonical Literature Their Own

The Nobel Prize Laureate and St. Lucian poet Derek Walcott (1998) has said, "The English language is nobody's special property. It is the property of the imagination" (p. 18). Students should be exposed to multicultural literature, but they should also have meaningful interactions with the Western canon. For example, W. B. Yeats's (1889) "The Stolen Child" inspired many of Gerald's students to describe the nostalgia they felt for their homelands while in the "fairyland" of the United States. Gerald also worked with secondary students to rewrite *Hamlet* as a bilingual script and set it in the context of American colonization of Puerto Rico.

Learn from and Provide Classroom Space for Students' Own Rich Storytelling Traditions

Refugee quilts are part of some students' family history. Stitched by hand, they illustrate flights from poverty and war and are found in such regions as the Andes, Afghanistan, and Southeast Asia. Some students may have talkstory as a tradition, the Hawaiian practice of sharing anecdotes through informal conversation. Some may be familiar with testimonial, a form of bearing witness to and documenting persecution and violence through firsthand accounts. Some may hail from African *griot*, or oral storytelling, traditions. In Gerald's classroom, the students performed stories about social issues relevant to their everyday lives using drama inspired by El Teatro Campesino, a tradition of political theater in migrant labor camps (Medina & Campano, 2006). As we describe further in Chapter 10, in conjunction with the Philadelphia Mural Arts Program, muralist and educator Eliseo Art Silva has developed innovative ways for children to reconstruct memory and tell visual stories through public art. For example, students dramatize scenes from their lives and bring in cultural artifacts from home that are visually incorporated into murals.

Incorporate Aspects of Popular Culture into the Classroom

Many young people are using alternative forms of creative expression, including visual art and music—such as underground hip-hop (Hill, 2009)—to innovatively convey their knowledge and engage in trenchant social commentary. In tracks such as "The Distance," the hip-hop duo the Blue Scholars speaks to the challenges, contradictions, and disillusionments of immigration. The lyrics and beat offer a counterstory to the conventional, triumphant immigrant narrative of upward mobility through hard work and sacrifice.

Literacy researchers (e.g., Duncan-Andrade & Morrell, 2005) have recently done groundbreaking research on the value of incorporating popular culture into the classroom. They point out the intellectual merit and sophistication found in many forms of youth cultural expression as well as the ways in which teachers can translate knowledge of popular culture into conventional academic standards and success. Students are also using mediums such as fan fiction, digital storytelling, and documentaries to individually and collectively narrativize their experiences. These primarily out-of school storying practices can be much more integrated into the regular school curriculum. For example, action researcher Lenny Sánchez has worked closely at the Boys Academy in Gary, Indiana (described in Chapter 2) with third graders who created documentaries investigating issues that they deemed important, such as poverty in the community and the history of the city's economic abandonment. In the documentaries, the children interviewed local experts, presented original research, and synthesized their findings through stories and rhyming.

Students can create digital stories that combine images, video, music, sounds, and text in multimodal productions that draw on popular culture material in ways that engage their audiences (Ohler, 2007), something we describe in more detail in Chapter 7.

Share Our Own Stories

Toni Morrison's Nobel Prize acceptance speech (1994) poignantly conveys the need for elders and teachers to make themselves vulnerable by passing down wisdom through narrative. She emphasizes this message through the tale of a blind woman who initially responds to the provocations of two young visitors, who ask her if the bird they have in their hands is alive or dead, with silence. The young people, in turn, respond by asking, "Is there no context for our lives? No song, no literature, no poem full of vitamins, no history connected to experience that you can pass along to help us start strong?" Morrison suggests that the young boys' acting out for attention was really a plea for wisdom. It is a reminder for educators not to hide behind their authority.

Teachers might, from time to time, step out of their institutional roles and share with students their own stories of struggle and change. For example, Gerald has shared with students that his own grandfather and father had to overcome deeply rooted inequality, such as antimiscegenation and Jim Crow laws, to provide for future generations. It was one of the ways by which his students were able to see their personal struggles as part of larger, ongoing legacies of dissent and social change. Sharing stories like this signals to students both the human and academic value of their own experiences.

Acknowledge Student Narratives as Intellectual Resources

Some of students' most powerful writing begins as oral stories told during unstructured academic time. In his fifth-grade classroom, Gerald invited his students to compose these more formally. This work often took place outside the confines of the mandated curriculum during "the second classroom" (Campano, 2007), pedagogical spaces on the margins of the school day—before school, after lunch, and at community events. Students need to know that their storied knowledge counts in school, is part of the intellectual dialogue of the classroom, and can serve as a departure point for further inquiry. Teachers can promote these understandings by continually communicating to students that their experiences matter.

Be Mindful That Stories Are Told Within Social and Political Contexts

Not all stories may be appropriate for all audiences. Some expose students to risk. For example, why would a child share her family's migrant narrative if she is worried that her parents might subsequently be deported? Or why would a student use his native language when it is frowned upon in school? Stories are a form of rhetoric. An important aspect of storytelling involves knowing what to say, how to say it, who to say it to, and in what situations and for what purposes. Teachers need to create safe spaces where students know their stories won't be used against them and feel empowered to create their own critical perspectives. As Dyson and Genishi (1994) note, "Stories, and thereby aspects of children's selves, can be silenced if listeners (including teachers and peers) do not appreciate the diverse ways stories are crafted and the range of experiences they tap" (p. 4). Our students' silences tell us as much as their words do about how schools may exclude their points of view (Carter, 2001).

Celebrate How Stories Represent Voices of Global Citizens Attempting to Make Change

Although schools tout the importance in their mission statements of preparing students for global citizenship, our youth are already global citizens. Many students, like Kendal, are able to analyze issues, such as prejudice or child labor, through a comparative cultural, and often transnational, framework. They have crisscrossed political borders and negotiated boundaries of race, class, generation, and gender. They have lived the consequences—both positive and negative—of globalization. Many have an intuitive grasp of injustice because they have experienced it firsthand. They are heirs to rich literacy and activist legacies. Narrative also has a speculative component helping students imagine a world free of domination (Solinger, Fox, & Irani, 2008). Wahid Omar (2008) recounts how young women in Jaghori, Afghanistan, created texts describing the persecution of their ethnic group, the Hazaras:

> This writer, like many of the young authors, wrote about injustice and racism in her story. After many vicissitudes, the story ends with the defeat of the evil warlord and justice is done. Our young Hazara storyteller uses a critical discourse in her story in order to counteract the mainstream Pashtun and Tajik discourse that degrades and belittles her people. (p. 198)

This blended genre transposes nonfiction accounts into heroic fictional narrative, enabling a minoritized community to imaginatively supersede its persecutions.

The deepest intellectual resources in classrooms are the students themselves. And one of the most powerful ways in which students can share their knowledge, partake in their own education, and intervene on their own behalf is by telling their stories.

Narratives therefore function as a powerful literacy tool to help students such as Kendal and his peers make sense of an often-complicated world by drawing on rich cultural storytelling traditions that have provided past generations with ways of understanding and explaining their lives. Furthermore, students use narratives to share their experiences with others to convey their particular identities and beliefs and establish their sense of agency as engaging storytellers who can make a difference in the world

FIVE

Dramatic Inquiry

Imagining and Enacting Life from Multiple Perspectives

> The big shift is to move from holding the information and doling it out like charity to creating the circumstances where it is imperative to inquire, search out, and interrogate the information we locate. If at present it isn't possible to merge the work of adults and the work of students because we don't value the contribution young children can bring to cultural development of the world's good, we can rely on proven drama systems to create "the mirror to nature" and harness, through identification and empathy, the life knowledge which children will bring generously to meet us half-way.
> —Dorothy Heathcote, *Real Players*, foreword, p. xii

In this chapter, we explore how teachers can use dramatic inquiry to extend a critical inquiry–based approach to literacy learning. Whereas much of teacher-mediated, improvised classroom drama's (Heathcote & Bolton, 1995) potential as a tool for literacy learning has been documented (Heath & Wolf, 2005; Schneider, Crumpler, & Rogers, 2007; Wagner, 1998), how it can contextualize inquiry-based dialogic curricular approaches has only begun to be recorded and theorized (Edmiston, 1998; Edmiston & Enciso, 2003), and its potential for extending student agency and shaping identities has only recently been considered (Edmiston, 2008).

Dramatic inquiry begins when adults participate in, and mediate, collaborative activities in the overlapping spaces of young people's inquiries and their dramatic improvisation. People of all ages may engage in the playful improvisation of dramatic inquiry. Dorothy Heathcote, who pioneered this approach, stressed the ubiquity and simplicity of dramatic activities: "the ability of humans to 'become somebody else,' to 'see how it feels' . . . to 'put yourself in my shoes' [is a capacity that] humans employ naturally and intuitively all their lives" (1984, p. 54). Dramatic inquiry harnesses that imaginative ability in order to deepen and extend students' inquiries. The following recent examples all come from schools in central Ohio:

- In a ninth-grade high school urban English classroom, students spoke as if on the telephone with their congressional representative, represented by Brian, to begin to explore their inquiry question: What might be done to help refugees in Darfur. Later, they deepened inquiries as they shifted perspective to imagine they were journalists, incognito, entering Sudan to document events and make them public.
- In a sixth-grade classroom in a Catholic school, young people explored why settlers and native people had not shared the land in Ohio 200 years previously. As if they were settlers, militia, and indigenous people, they improvised interactions and made decisions about attacks, possible retaliation, and resettlement as Brian mediated their collaborative movement among, and interpretation of, different perspectives on historical events referred to only in passing in their social studies textbook.
- In a fourth-grade classroom at an arts lottery urban school, African American and European American children imagined they were with Bessie Coleman, the first Black female aviator, when they encountered Brian, who blocked their way as if he were the White owner of a flight school in the 1920s; later they discussed how people then and now can act in the face of discrimination.

In this chapter we use examples from two suburban central Ohio settings: a fifth-grade classroom in an elementary school, and two first-grade classrooms in New Albany K–1 School. The use of examples from first-grade classrooms in a book with a grade 5–12 audience might seem surprising. However, because Brian co-taught over a school year in those classrooms, those examples illustrate how identities and agency can shift when dramatic inquiry is used over longer periods of time to shape classroom spaces.

We use examples from these classrooms to illustrate the significance for students' agency and identity formation when adults create with young people imagined spaces for inquiry via dramatic improvisation. First, we illustrate how young people identify with an emerging community of literacy practices in which students who improvise in playful imagined spaces can become more competent at collaboratively using extensive multimodal literacy tools. Second, we demonstrate how adult mediation of dramatic inquiry activities, in particular positioning students as competent and capable in dramatic performances, are tools that affect classroom power relationships, the construction of more dialogic understandings, and the identities of both young people and teachers.

DRAMATIC INQUIRY AS A LITERACY TOOL-OF-TOOLS

Because people experience the spaces of dramatic inquiry as if they were real, we argue that dramatic inquiry is not a single literacy tool but rather, like language itself, is an educational "tool of tools" (Cole, 1996). Teachers can use the multiple intersecting tools of dramatic inquiry to transform classrooms into spaces for literacy learning and teaching that not only create opportunities for composing and interpreting texts but also extend critical inquiry, foster students' agency, and promote development of their perspectives.

During the 2007–08 school year Janie Sammons and Trish Russell regularly used the critical literacy tools of dramatic inquiry. The young people in Janie's and Trish's classes imagined that they had the responsibility for running travel agencies. Toward the end of the year, in Janie's classroom, as the first-grade children planned an imagined trip to Rwanda for conservationists as if they were members of the Extreme Adventures Travel Agency, at different times they considered how to greet people from another culture, how people there lived, and how they could be assisted to reduce their environmental impact and thus better protect local mountain gorillas.

Meanwhile, inquiries in Trish's class focused on vacations on the ocean off the coast of Florida. After carefully planning successful and safe trips, as if they were members of Exciting Water Adventures, to "swim with dolphins," the first graders critiqued adult decisions as they invented what happened to an injured client when another company, Scuba Adventures, had not been very safety-conscious.

In Sarah Higgins's classroom 3 years previously over a 90-minute period, fifth-grade students adopted the perspectives of sculptors creating a sculpture to pose a critical inquiry question: From whose perspectives should the Thanksgiving story be told? The young people read and critiqued accounts from different viewpoints both on paper and as represented by visiting adults depicting historical people. As they wrote, sketched, and presented ideas, while participating in heated discussions, the young people reexamined some of their prior assumptions about Thanksgiving.

For Janie, using dramatic inquiry revitalized students' involvement in an annual schoolwide "Partners in Conservation" event planned for May

2008. As Janie noted, "For the first time the children cared about, had an understanding of why we were involved in this project, and took on responsibility. They didn't want to stop working on it." Presenters from the local zoo would annually visit classrooms in this suburban school to tell the mostly affluent children about the zoo's involvement in a Rwandan project. As students they normally had little to do beyond listen as they were informed about how money gathered at fund-raisers would be used to purchase and deliver goats, stoves, and bicycles to East Africa. But this year was different. They enacted the presentations of the goats that would provide milk and could forage in the forest, unlike cattle, which need pasture in cleared land; they pretended to cook as they drew pictures of the stoves that burn less fuel than open fires, reducing the need for wood that they imagined gathering from the forest; and some imagined riding on rough terrain the bicycles that provide transportation and relaxed the pressure to migrate to cities or poach in the protected forest.

The following fieldnotes, written toward the end of the year and after several weeks working on the Partners in Conservation project, illustrate how after months of dramatic inquiry activities the classroom had been transformed into a space where students, assisted by adults, were actively and collaboratively making meaning as they moved back and forth between discussion and dramatic improvisation. These young children both played and performed as they dramatically explored questions about their relationship with Rwanda.

> The students sit with Brian to read an illustrated children's book about Swahili, one of the official languages of Rwanda: *Jambo Means Hello* (Feelings, 1992) is an A–Z book with English commentary. Talking as if he too is a travel agent, Brian raises questions about what words they might use on their Rwandan trip and how they might greet people respectfully. As they listen, several boys who had been making drums collaboratively continue to work on them using rubber bands, cloth, and containers. Then, to illustrate the Swahili word for drum, Brian asks the boys to play as the other children respond with great enthusiasm. He wonders if the people in Rwanda might like to hear them playing their own drums; the children think so. Soon, many more children are making and playing drums and other instruments and inventing names for their musical creations. Some children return to the book for Swahili words that they adapt. Colin retrieves a previously written story and begins to revise it while some consult books previously gathered by the classroom teacher. Some cluster round a visiting teacher's laptop

looking for information about Rwanda. Others, assisted by Janie and other visiting adults in the classroom, try out possible ways of cross-cultural greeting including dance and singing while John creates a surveillance camera to check for the poachers they knew could be in the area. Children then gather to present their ideas to one another, and to the three visiting teachers, as all engage in discussion around the inquiry question: How should we greet people in Rwanda?

Dramatic inquiry dramatizes whole-class inquiries about life. The above example illustrates our use of the term dramatic inquiry: embodied, collaborative, interactive, and sequenced improvised activities that young people engage in alongside adults as they explore questions about a topic from multiple viewpoints by creating, experiencing, representing, and interpreting socially imagined events as if they are actually happening here and now. Like the improvised interactions in spontaneous dramatic play and unscripted staged dramatic performances, but unlike the many largely prescribed individualized events in young people's lives in school, the activities of dramatic inquiry both create and then occur in socially imagined spaces that resemble everyday life experiences. At the same time, forming depicted events in dramatic inquiry creates significance in the sense that "all the ideas embodied . . . are considered by the group to be relevant" (Heathcote, 1984, p. 55).

In Trish Russell's classroom the students reconsidered "safety" as they imagined the consequences of the unsafe practices of Scuba Adventures. Trish and Brian led adult-mediated whole-group dramatic playing, with children taking turns as if they were attacking as, and being attacked by, sharks and other dangerous sea creatures the children had researched. With much laughter they delighted at shifting informally into brief collaborative dramatic performances that showed what could have happened as swimmers were overpowered by attacking creatures.

With adult assistance the children formed their ideas: everything shown was relevant to their ongoing inquiry into how to be safe. Older students could have jumped straight into shaping and showing the still images that Trish captured on digital photographs as the younger children held a pose of "the most dangerous moments" in the stories they invented. Having printed out the images, each student then used markers to draw individually imagined events around each photograph. And after Trish talked with the children-as-reporters, each interpreted events as they wrote an accompanying story as if retold by a reporter for the local newspaper.

In Sarah Higgins's fifth-grade classroom, imagining they were sculptors designing a Thanksgiving commemorative monument, the students took up a critical inquiry stance as they encountered, explored, dramatized, and critiqued different perspectives on the 1620 historical events. Sarah began by reading them a letter as if from a federal group, the National Monument Association, written to a group of sculptors who had been commissioned to design a monument commemorating Thanksgiving. Like the younger students who had eagerly imagined they had the responsibility of travel agents, these older students created and entered an imagined space as if they were adult designers with expertise. The first graders had been eager to move and interact as if they were travel agents as well as villagers and gorillas in Rwanda or sharks and swimmers in the ocean; during their short introduction to the pedagogy of dramatic inquiry, the fifth graders more gradually interacted in imagined spaces. Initially, they talked with Sarah as a fellow sculptor, and all participated in reading a letter and in response made and then shared publicly their drawings of possible designs. Later, they gained new perspectives by talking with visiting adults who dramatized their historical research by performing as if they were the historical Plymouth governor, Edward Winslow, and the indigenous leaders, Squanto and Massasoit. Finally, they imagined that they were modern-day Wampanoag people debating whether to celebrate Thanksgiving or participate in the National Day of Mourning.

IMAGINED-AND-REAL SPACES

Because people create spaces as they interact, Leander and Sheehy (2004) have argued that classroom literacy learning should be "spatialized." Lefebrve (1991) theorized that life is lived, experienced, and understood in socially produced, but dynamically changing, "real-and-imagined spaces" that have histories and futures as well as present geographies. Everyday life is imagined in the sense that social and cultural norms have no objective physical reality but have been, and continue to be, socially constructed and conceptualized in mental images that are made visible in predictable social interactions. What was, and is, imagined acquires a reality for people when they participate in social practices that they accept are how people ought to act in particular situations, for example how one person greets another in a particular time and place.

We argue that dramatic inquiry inverts the experience of everyday life by creating social "imagined-and-real spaces" for the purposes of critical and dialogic inquiry. In dramatic inquiry, socially imagined events and possibilities become visible in embodied action in a social space that is experienced by participants as if it is actually elsewhere: in a travel agency, in Rwanda, or in Plymouth in 1620. Additionally, social relationships and hierarchies may be playfully shaped and changed in ways that could not actually happen in everyday life, as people pretend to act as if they are other persons. Students' participation over time in activities in the spaces of dramatic inquiry creates a fictionalized "drama world" (O'Neill, 1995) that overlaps with the everyday classroom world. Inverting the experience of the everyday, in dramatic inquiry what is socially imagined in the moment is foregrounded while everyday reality is backgrounded. In ways similar to when young children engage in spontaneous dramatic play, as Vygotsky (1967) realized, the symbolic meaning of people's social actions and any objects they use as multimodal tools become more important than the actual actions and objects themselves. This reversal is significant because, as Vygotsky stressed, "play leads development": in the enacted playful social imagination of dramatic inquiry, children learn in meaningful situations how to use language and other tools, to create abstracted symbolic meaning, for example, the meanings of greeting in different settings are abstractions situated in and formed from particular concrete situations.

By extension, when people of any age engage in the dramatic improvisation of dramatic inquiry, they learn to use and understand more of the conceptual meaning created by multimodal literacy tools in diverse but particular social and cultural situations. In Janie's classroom, adults as well as children thought about the intercultural dimensions of communication in and about Rwanda. As Janie noted, "It was so much fun dancing with the girls, but I'd not really thought about how a dance might be a great thing to do to connect with people in another country until I joined in and then talked about it when we shared with everyone." In the spaces of dramatic inquiry activities, to paraphrase Soja (1996), physical, mental, emotional, and social tools are seen as simultaneously imagined and real, concrete and abstract material and metaphorical. Janie was adamant that for her students just abstractly talking about the Rwandan project had been neither engaging nor educational the previous year. Since the children had already been imagining that they were travel agents as if at a planning meeting, Janie and Brian suggested to them-as-travel-agents, "How about we take on a new project?" The interest of the class in planning a trip to Rwanda for conservationists was aroused as they watched, on the classroom smartboard, video clips from the Internet showing local farmers at work, deforestation, and images of the national park where mountain gorillas live. The smartboard presentation was made by Camille Cushman, a graduate student participant-observer, and facilitated by Brian. By making the interactive presentation as if she were one of the travel agents' potential clients (a person who had just returned from Rwanda, who wanted us as travel agents to plan a trip for the group from the Partners in Conservation project she had agreed to lead), Camille could give focused and personal responses that both gave information and raised newly contextualized professional questions among the young people: Why had people cut down trees? Did gorillas hide? Would the rangers use their guns to shoot people? Inquiry questions such as these focused the adult-assisted children's improvisations that followed.

DRAMATIC IMPROVISATION

In dramatic inquiry, improvisation comes to the fore, as it does in the online role-play activities we describe in Chapter 7. As Robinson (2001) characterizes it, improvisation is creative "applied imagination" rather than flights of fancy, for example applied toward appropriate use of language and movement when participating in particular social situations. In online role-play young people learn literacy by improvised participation in the engaging imagined spaces of a virtual game world using a class blog or social networking site as described in Chapter 7. In dramatic inquiry young people, along with participating adults, similarly improvise in imagined spaces, but they do so by moving and interacting as if they are actually in newly imagined scenarios that may both tap into students' interests, knowledge, and cultural resources as well as meet teachers' particular literacy goals. For example, the first-grade students in Janie's classroom, working alongside supportive adults who asked questions and pressed for new possibilities, used their prior knowledge of the social practices of greeting, online information from the Web and books about Rwanda, as well as their prior writing, to raise questions and explore possibilities about how to greet people in Rwanda as they moved, talked, read, wrote, and made music to explore possible respectful cross-cultural greetings: Would a handshake be appropriate? A smile? Gifts? A story? What sort of music and dance?

Though all dramatic improvisation is collaborative and unscripted, some dramatic inquiry activities focus more on the shared experience of *participating* in imagined-and-real social practices, while other activities are more concerned with some people performing ideas to *communicate* with an imagined audience. Both are significant from a literacy learning viewpoint: literacy is learned both by participating in the literacy practices of a community and by using language to create texts to communicate with others. Dramatic improvisation that is mostly about imaginatively experiencing other people's social practices is called *dramatic playing* (e.g., moving as if we were gorillas foraging in a forest, travel agents consulting maps to plan trips, or sculptors using clay to design a monument). Improvisation that is mostly about the presentation and interpretation of events from the imagined lives of other people is a *dramatic performance* (e.g., a conservationist showing and commenting on a slide show about gorilla habitats to travel agents, agents planning and making a phone call to a client, or sculptors sharing and explaining a design with colleagues). Unlike stage performers, who expect applause, but like everyday life, the audience for a dramatic inquiry performance is not external to the group (Bolton, 1999).

Rather than being different types of activity, dramatic play and dramatic performance can be considered different objectives of activities that can be placed on a dramatic improvisation continuum depending on the extent of people's embodied movement as if acting as other people in an imagined space. At one end of the continuum lies the sort of open-ended active playful movement that most young children engage in spontaneously, that many actors employ in rehearsals, but that takes most older students and adults longer to become comfortable with. Toward the middle lies more focused creations, for example, brief still images in a tableau. At the other end of the continuum lie informal conversations where people only minimally use their bodies to represent other people; these are the sorts of activities that older school students and adults initially tend to find most comfortable. All improvised activities are playful when people imagine they are elsewhere, and all become performances when there is a presentation that is interpreted by watchers.

In Sarah's fifth-grade classroom the students were comfortable with participation that required only minimal embodiment in imagined times and places. Though the students' dramatic improvisations were more conversational than physically embodied, they were still both playful and performative. Sarah initially performed as a sculptor reading a letter to promote a conversation with the students-as-sculptors focused on the question of from whose perspectives the Thanksgiving story should be told. Later, visiting graduate students gave information and answered questions as if they were paintings of historical characters that came alive so that the students could interact with them. In doing so, they could interpret both as themselves and later as if they were contemporary Wampanoag people at a council meeting as they considered whether to celebrate Thanksgiving or participate in the National Day of Mourning.

The young children in Janie's classroom were both generally more active and more experienced using the tools of dramatic inquiry. Rather than just use talk to create a shared understanding of the class project, the children readily engaged in active playful improvisation that dramatized, applied, and extended information they had gained from books and the Web. Camille, Janie, and Brian pretended with the children to be walking in a forest. After dimming the lights and moving the tables and chairs, they made forest sounds together and imagined seeing, hearing, and briefly being animals and plants. And then, to explore the consequences of poaching, as they talked about a construction paper representation of an animal trap that poachers used to catch gorillas, Brian moved into a brief performance. Whereas the historical characters in Sarah's classroom had been mostly static as they were interviewed, Brian narrated a story as he moved his arm along the carpet to enact a baby gorilla's movement through the forest and its hand being caught when it stepped on a hidden trap. This activity was embedded into an ongoing discussion about the project. As travel agents, the children's interpretation and response to the enacted story was clear: they wanted to save the gorillas and organize an imagined trip to Rwanda. The students were eager to participate in interviews during additional informal presentations by Camille (as the returned conservationist), as well as by Janie and Brian (as representatives from the zoo). Soon groups were planning, creating, and sharing illustrated plans that some tried out in dramatic play. Most drew, and with adult direction, informally shared with others about how they would move through the forest and bring goats, stoves, and bicycles to the local people.

AGENCY IN
DRAMATIC INQUIRY

People enact agency in the improvisation of dramatic inquiry that would be difficult or impossible to experience or maintain in their everyday lives. As they dramatize struggling with shared objectives, the multimodal literacy tools available to students are extended in socially imagined spaces.

In 90 minutes the students in Sarah Higgins's fifth-grade classroom used drawings; their responses to adults' dramatic performances; limited movement; and their talk in the imagined-and-real spaces of sculptors, the historical time of 1620, and a meeting of contemporary Native Americans. From multiple perspectives, the students explored the question of whether to celebrate or mourn Thanksgiving. Though this was the first time she had used dramatic inquiry with her students, Sarah recognized its power to extend student agency.

It was amazing. Students who, in the everyday classroom, were shy and hesitant to speak, were able to take up positions and voice their ideas confidently. Nick was a particularly shy student who rarely spoke up in class and did not like to draw attention to himself. When they were imagining that they were Wampanoag council members, Nick spoke up and challenged his classmates to reconsider their previous unquestioned assumption [that all Americans should celebrate Thanksgiving] apparent in their initial stereotypical drawings of Indians and Pilgrims sharing turkey: "They [the Pilgrims] were probably glad they destroyed us. They're probably not going to care. I think what we should do is not celebrate Thanksgiving and have our own version of Thanksgiving."

Over several months, the children in Janie Sammons's first-grade classroom had opportunities to extend their agency in dramatic improvisation. Using a range of literacy tools that included images and ideas from adults, books, and the Internet, as well as drawings, maps, writing, movements, sounds, and interactions, they transformed the everyday classroom not only into a travel agency where they could explore how to keep people safe in extreme situations but also into other imagined-and-real spaces that included the multifaceted landscape in Rwanda. Over time, there were opportunities for all students to extend their agency. John was preceived to be a student who often engaged in parallel play and whose ideas were discounted. His agency, and how his peers saw him, was transformed when he stood on a chair to use the surveillance camera he had made so that people could watch for poachers. Janie commented:

When we started showing the camera and what was happening down there everyone in the room stopped doing what they were doing. Even though they were really interested in that, they then saw John standing on that chair pretending he had the camera looking down. I remember all the dancers had stopped and they were all looking. He was the king for a moment; he was hardly ever the king.

The students' agency over time created socially imagined worlds that transformed how they acted every day. Because the children agreed that adult travel agents would not have meetings controlled by a single adult where they would raise hands, new collaborative ways of listening and building on ideas were negotiated, for example passing round a "talking stick" and taking turns to draw ideas on the smartboard.

CRITICAL, DIALOGIC, DRAMATIC INQUIRY

Dramatic inquiry can create spaces where young people's agency to act is confronted with actions and voices coming from viewpoints they had not previously considered.

At one point in the Rwandan project, the children hid from and then encountered Brian-as-a-poacher, setting a trap. He justified his action in an accompanying narrative about his hungry family and how he would make more money from selling a gorilla than he could make in a year as a farmer. The children challenged this belief as they physically surrounded Brian. When one of the children said, "Traps kill gorillas. They have a right to live, too," the other children were in agreement, though one added quietly, "But he needs to feed his family." In the dramatic improvisation the young people were critically engaged with a complex problem they would never actually encounter that also challenged their initial assumption that no one should kill a gorilla.

Brian's adult mediation created a space that for some became more dialogic as well as critical: the embodied ideas young people defined in the poacher space were placed in dialogue with understanding they had created in the prior space of the baby gorillas that needed saving from the traps. The understanding created in the exchange was more dialogic for children who had projected into and considered action from both viewpoints (Bakhtin, 1981). With older students, this project could have dialogically critiqued potentially colonizing attitudes of Western "help," made visible the colonial roots of the region's genocide, and exposed non-African economic demands that contribute to central African environmental degradation.

Adult-mediated activities in the spaces of dramatic inquiry over time promoted more dialogic conceptual explorations. For example, one of the agreed principles of the travel agency arose from a discussion about what the word "extreme" meant in the contexts of all the possible trips they might provide. It was agreed that though vacations could feel dangerous and involve sensible risks, they would always be "fun and safe." What "safety" meant then became one of the ongoing inquiry questions that had no easy answers but was explored in different contexts: designing movable cages for people to keep them safe from jaguars; safety for gorillas and people in the presence of traps; and explaining to conservationists what to do in the forest because there might be poachers.

The Rwandan project was critical inquiry focused on promoting social justice for both gorillas and local people. In previous years its focus had been mostly information-gathering. In Sarah Higgins's fifth-grade classroom the Thanksgiving inquiry was initially focused by a critical question: From whose perspectives should the story be told? After reading and then encountering and engaging in dialogue with viewpoints from 1620, the students all agreed that indigenous perspectives had to be included. Sarah now posed a more difficult question: Should we continue to celebrate Thanksgiving as we have always done, or like many contemporary indigenous and nonindigenous people, should we participate in the National Day of Mourning? The students-as-contemporary-Wampanoags were asked to reinterpret their previous stereotypical drawings. Sarah noted that Xavier's ideas made a difference.

> In the imagined space Xavier's contributions were very relevant, and many moved the class from just imagining different perspectives to critical dialogue that challenged stereotypes and misconceptions of the traditional Thanksgiving story. Imagining that he was a contemporary Wampanoag, Xavier was passionate in declaring that indigenous people and the pilgrims were not friends who sat down to have dinner. His comments opened up a critical discussion about whether the past should dictate our actions in the present.

As the students-as-sculptors revised their initial stereotypical sketches, they became both more dialogic and critical.

> *Mary*: I can't decide what to make the sculpture look like. Only because if we do the sculpture how the Indians want it, then it won't represent how we do it. And if we do how we want it then the Indians will be mad.
> *Steve*: I think the sculpture should have four sides, one with the first Thanksgiving, one with an Indian and a Pilgrim with half of the treaty, one with a plaque and one with modern Thanksgiving.
> *Xavier*: I would show a sculpture of a peace treaty but behind the sculpture a war scene.

Over time, if these fifth-grade students had become as comfortable using the multimodal tools of dramatic inquiry as the first graders, they could have engaged in a more extensive dialogic exploration. For example, in creating, interpreting, and revising small- and whole-group still images of sculpture designs, the students could have taken up and engaged in dialogue from multiple viewpoints across time and space.

DRAMATIC INQUIRY IS A LITERACY OF POSSIBILITIES

Karen Wohlwend (2008) convincingly argues that dramatic play is a multimodal "literacy of possibilities" that "expands meanings in practices, materials, and spaces." Both play and performance in dramatic inquiry are highly significant for learning, and literacy learning in particular, because young people are learning social practices using tools that are in advance of what they would or could use in everyday life. As Vygotsky (1967) put it, in play it is as if people are "a head taller": they may have the authority to use a phone or fly a plane combined with the responsibility to interview a client or write a report. As the first-grade children invented their travel agency, they created agendas and procedures for team meetings and ways of speaking on the phone and interviewing clients, and they planned and shared countless imagined ideas in action, online, and on paper.

When people play they can try out and perform new identities, or as Marcus and Nurius (1986) might word it, have the agency to act as other "possible selves" in imagined spaces. In dramatic inquiry students can experiment with alternative identifications that are foregrounded over everyday identities. In dramatic inquiry young people are no longer tied to established student identities but can participate in collaborative community practices as other possible selves trying out different identities. Possible selves and identities will be shaped by the "epistemic frame" (Shaffer, 2006) of whatever "enterprise" of expertise (Heathcote & Bolton, 1995) they collectively imagine running: sculptors, travel agents, and so on. As Shaffer (2006) puts it, the shared epistemic frame provides "the ways of knowing, of deciding what is worth knowing, and of adding to the collective body of knowledge and understanding of a community of practice."

The children in first grade had months to become more competent and knowledgeable participants in the imagined-and-real communities that developed. In addition to travel agencies, the young people in the SAIL classrooms created communities of scuba divers, hospitals, Nocturnal Wildlife Park Rangers, the helpers who helped Goldilocks, Humpty Dumpty, and a fishing community on a tropical island damaged in a hurricane. Their identities could change as they repeatedly took on responsibilities in these imagined-and-real communities. As Janie put it: "You can expect more out of them and they expect more out of themselves because they're not [just] seven-year-olds or six-year-olds. They're adults creating something for other people. Their responsibility is greater, I mean, they're doing something for other people. This is their job and they're really good at it."

Mark's changing identity became a touchstone for Janie's developing understanding of the power of dramatic inquiry. At the beginning of the year, Mark often impulsively blurted out imaginative ideas, which were marginalized by peers and regarded by Janie as often "inappropriate." Yet, in the context of the activities and practices of the travel agency, Mark's improvised ideas could become central. Midway through the year his invention of a cage to protect humans from jaguars became a turning point when this idea inspired other students, who engaged in dramatic improvisation about using, and actually constructing, protective devices to take on safari. As Janie noted, "It was not just the children who began to see Mark differently. I did, too. He had become a member of our community." By the end of the year Mark socially participated in multiple ways. In the Rwandan example he contributed but never blurted out ideas, joined in with a group making a drum, later moved his body rhythmically when possible music was shared by others, and listened when a story was told. Janie stressed how he had changed: "He wasn't that kid at the beginning of the year when everyone was doing this and rolling their eyes. He wasn't that person anymore. He was that person, 'Wooh, what's he going to say?' And then they were able to talk to him about it and he was able to change his ideas, which he would have never done."

In dramatic inquiry, an epistemic frame is not given but is created over time through ongoing interactions and social practices. New identities only form when students have the agency to engage in new practices over days and months. In all SAIL classrooms the children eagerly chose to take on responsibility for collaboratively grappling with social problems. They regularly brought in artifacts and information from home, and many parents reported on how reading, research, and play continued out of school with friends. In Trish Russell's classroom, the children wrote letters at the end of the year to their prospective second-grade teachers filled with extended narratives, retellings, references to social interactions, and their pleasure at pretending and imagining the world differently. All but one letter focused mostly on their dramatic inquiries and pointed to identities that contrasted with the dominant individualistic school discourse. These comments (with corrected spellings) were typical:

> *Peter*: It is fun to pretend to go to different places all around the
> world. I went to the rain forest and the ocean. I got to study
> dolphins. I got to pretend to be a dolphin. I liked when we made
> an ocean out of paper.
>
> *Julie*: I liked it when my friends Lilly and Susan helped me understand
> a hard problem.
>
> *Tina*: I like pretending to be a nurse. . . . We are being people in the
> hospital because someone [Bruce Foster] got bit by a shark. We

are trying to help him get better. We are also seeing if we have to shut down Scuba Adventures. I hope we don't have to. I want to keep it safe.

Trish's summarizing comments point to a comparison of students' iden-tification with community practices at the end of one year with the previous year: "Usually they write a few lines and say things like 'I like recess. I like math.' But never about anything that happened in the classroom and never with this sort of detail. Many of these letters are their longest pieces of writ-ing ever. They're filled with the language of what 'we' did. They just brought tears to my eyes. I felt like the children had been making memories to take with them."

Though young people's identities as community members change over time when they have repeated opportunities to collaborate as competent, knowledgeable participants in the spaces of whatever drama worlds are cre-ated, Sarah's comments about fifth graders Nick and Xavier suggest that students using dramatic inquiry may begin to identify differently in a very short period of time.

Nick was usually a quiet student. In the dramatic inquiry he contributed, made comments, and engaged in conversations that were unusual for him in the classroom. Xavier often positioned himself as an outsider by distancing himself from his peers in the everyday classroom. Yet, in the imagined space he could share his thoughts in a space where he was heard. In his reflection he wrote, "In drama class I felt cool and a part of the group. It helped me learn better."

DRAMATIC INQUIRY IS A LITERACY OF POWER RELATIONSHIPS

When adults foster a critical awareness of how power operates in social relationships, a literacy of possibilities may become a literacy of power re-lationships. Critical inquiry questions can be contextualized in engaging imagined-and-real spaces of dramatic inquiry, focused on power relation-ship, and explored by students in improvised activities that are both playful and performative. Adult participation can focus inquiry, shape activities, and dialogically extend understanding.

In Sarah Higgins's classroom, critical inquiry questions were contextual-ized in the imagined task she negotiated with her students: a group of sculp-tors were charged with designing a sculpture to commemorate Thanksgiving.

The dramatic performances by her and visiting adults presented alternative perspectives to the stereotypical ones assumed by the students' textbook and revealed in their initial drawings. The students encountered some of the silenced voices in the Thanksgiving story, for example, that the indigenous people kept the Pilgrims alive but were then attacked by the English, who broke the 1621 peace treaty. However, it was only when the inquiry question was dramatically tightened to focus on choosing between designing a statue that celebrated or mourned Thanksgiving that the students-as-Wampanoags revisited their designs and began to comment on their perception of their power to shape different interpretations. The following exchange between Xavier and John illustrates different assumptions of the young people:

> *Xavier*: People think we got along and they want to put up a statue of us getting along, we did NOT get along.
> *John*: You really can't change what happened in the past. The past is the past. [He added later:] We're here and we're alive and that's all in the past and we're doing fine so we should just let it go.
> *Xavier*: But you can change it now. You can change the past now so in the future. . . . [He added later:] I would show a sculpture of a peace treaty but behind the sculpture a war scene.

John regarded the past as unchangeable events that should be let go, whereas Xavier assumed that he had some power to shape people's future interpretations about the meaning of the past. He was adamant that images of war had to accompany images based on the traditional discourse that Thanksgiving was an idyllic peace.

In Trish Russell's first-grade classroom, she and Brian had more time to use the tools of dramatic inquiry to make visible and explore with students how power circulates and can be supported or contested in relation to other people (Foucault, 1980): the power of a Safety Commission to shut down a travel company and the power of people in a hospital to save a person's life. In the spaces of dramatic inquiry, the children took on responsibility for using power within those relationships as they improvised responses to critical inquiry questions: Should Scuba Adventures be closed? How will the patient be cared for?

In dramatic improvisation the young people had imagined and critiqued the shark attack experience from the viewpoints of a victim, the sharks, and the journalists retelling the story. Additionally, many of the children eagerly set up and, as if they were physicians and nurses, played with running the hospital where Bruce Foster, who had been bitten by a shark, was in intensive care. As they created and labeled representations of medical equipment, tended sick patients, and kept records, they experienced the incident from the viewpoints of professional caregivers, many of whom on several occasions (in informal dramatic performances) reported to Trish-as-Bruce's-mother his fluctuating condition and all they were doing to save him despite the many medical challenges they invented.

On a subsequent day, after many of the young people read from their prominently displayed shark attack stories, Trish, Brian, Mary Beth Ressler (another graduate student participant-observer), and a visiting mother of one of the children gave a more formal dramatic performance of a prepared, but also improvised and interactive, scenario that represented what had happened after Bruce Foster had been attacked; it was designed to contextualize their inquiries in a dramatization of multiple laminated spaces of power relationships. Brian began by standing beside and reading an adult-written sign for "SCUBA ADVENTURES: WE TAKE YOU WHERE NO ONE ELSE WILL GO" attached to the end of a bookcase. He had a "CLOSED TEMPORARILY" sign written in red ink in his hand. As Brian narrated what happened to the shark attack victim and how the company had been closed down, he firmly attached the sign. Standing nearby, a shocked-looking Mary Beth was introduced reading the adult-created front page of the *Florida Times* newspaper with the clearly visible headline "SHARK ATTACK." Brian read the headline with the children and then mediated a brief interview with Mary Beth-as-the-reader who told how the company took people to "swim with sharks." Mary Beth-as-a-news-reporter then interviewed a distraught Trish-as-Bruce-Foster's-mother, who was in the waiting room at the hospital looking at adult-created charts that showed fluctuating vital signs. Trish fielded questions from the children, who wanted to know how her son was being cared for. Finally, a very serious-looking Carol-as-Florida-Safety-Commissioner was introduced. She asked the children what should be done about Scuba Adventures. The children wanted to know who she was, and in a discussion about what a safety commissioner might do they agreed that some people had to have the power to stop others from being unsafe. Several children said Scuba Adventures should be closed down. Pointing to the red sign, Brian asked whether it should be closed "temporarily" or "forever." After explaining the word temporarily, their monologic opinion was clear: No one thought it should be reopened. A dictated red sign was added: "CLOSED FOREVER."

Three weeks later, though Trish had reported that the children were finished with the Bruce Foster narrative, when Brian arrived David approached him, saying, "Bruce Foster is still in intensive care." When a space was created for David to speak and address the whole class, it was clear that the children were keen to return to the story. Within moments the hospital had been reestablished, with David-as-Dr.-Bloodsector checking on the patient's vital signs and Joan drawing a new chart showing that his blood pressure was now normal.

Ten minutes later, having gathered the children together, Brian-as-the-safety-commissioner asked the children if they would like to imagine that they also worked on the commission and could make the final decision about what should happen to Scuba Adventures. They were keen to do that, but unsure what to do. When Brian-as-the-safety-commissioner said that maybe all water adventure vacation companies should be shut down as just too dangerous. It was a serious Ansel who said that this would have to include Exciting Water Adventures (the enterprise they had previously imagined running), and everyone heard that in a moment of stillness that signaled assent. To introduce another viewpoint, Brian moved back to the "CLOSED FOREVER" sign. Brian-as-Scuba-Adventures-owner said how sorry he was about Bruce Foster, promised to do whatever he could to make amends, but begged them not to shut him down because he had no money left in the bank. Moving toward the children, Brian intended to position them with a skeptical view on the owner's appeal, but power had flowed to the owner and the dominant voice (that Ansel endorsed) was that he should be given another chance.

In a brief 5-minute meeting, as if they were safety commissioners, only a few of the children still monologically wanted to shut down Scuba Adventures. They had a more complex awareness of the power relationships. After several views had been heard, and Trish-as-Bruce-Foster's-mother was asked what she thought (she wanted no one to get hurt again), one person suggested that there should be safety rules, and no one was opposed to drafting official commission rules. Though there was no time on that day to enact what would happen, many wanted to write a concluding story. Everyone agreed that Scuba Adventures could reopen, but only when the owner showed that he would follow rules that would keep everyone safe, with no exceptions.

PERFORMING POSSIBLE SELVES AND CHANGING IDENTITIES

In the performances of everyday classroom spaces there is an everyday power relationship between presenters and audience that affects the authority of people to control events and their interpretation. Adults (who tend to position themselves as presenters in authority) and young people (who tend to be positioned as an audience with little authority) can settle into predictable relationships and patterns of interaction in which over time the subjectivities, or social positions, of "teacher" and "students" are constructed; from a relational viewpoint, these become people's primary or fallback classroom identities.

However, the identities of teachers and students can change. After a year of using dramatic inquiry, Janie saw herself in a very different relationship with the young people in her classroom.

> You actually see their excitement in learning and that's what teachers want to do. Teachers want to see kids who want to learn. Teachers want to see kids learning. That's what dramatic inquiry did. Not only academically. It's fun to see kids talking together and working in a group. And getting something done that's cool for everybody. I think, for me, it really was looking at children differently. Honestly. Truly different. This way, there's no supposed to, have to, you're wrong, there's no wrong way because they're different and they're being them. You don't have expectations of them to be a certain person. They can be whoever they want to be.

Drama literacy tools enable teachers to "look differently" at young people who are silenced or marginalized in the conventional standardized school curriculum. In Trish Russell's classroom Joan would talk over others while David, who had cerebral palsy, tended not to speak in public. Some may experience a deeply alienated position: Ansel, at the beginning of the year, had a highly oppositional relational identity. He was regularly in the principal's office for aggressive behavior toward others, had difficulty collaborating with peers, and said he had no friends and hated school.

In dramatic performances, social positions shift when children and adults take on different possible selves. Over time, everyday positional identities can also be transformed: young people can become more than their prior largely predictable identity as "students" and adults more than "teachers." In the imagined-and-real spaces of dramatic performances, adults can radically affect how young people position their selves and one another in the classroom community. Students with previous low status and little power can be positioned with higher authority to act and interpret events in spaces with a common frame of shared responsibility. Over the year, as well as pretending to be other people or creatures (includes sharks and bats), with support Ansel took on collaborative authority within the group as various possible selves (as a bus driver, a gatherer of other people's opinions, a creator of images, a sharer of information from books, and a person fielding questions). His drawing abilities, his imagination, and his content knowledge all came to the fore as much as possible, interpreted as "for us" within spaces where he could choose how to participate in activities. Over the same time,

Joan became someone who waited more often before talking, and David became someone who would speak, when it became clear to both of them that everyone's ideas would be heard and used and that no one could dominate in the collaborative spaces in which they were included. And Trish's desire to share more power with children was also realized as she took on multiple supportive possible selves in the drama worlds (e.g., as a reporter, a mother, and a hospital administrator) and came to position children differently. She summarized her changing identity: "Not only do you teach them how to be creative and how to incorporate language arts but also how to be real people and to feel like they're going to be somebody in the world."

DRAMATIC INQUIRY AS COLLABORATIVE SOCIAL IMAGINATION

Maxine Greene (1996) insists that use of social imagination, collaboratively grounded in the lives of adults and young people, is central to learning and critical inquiry.

> The classroom situation most provocative of thoughtfulness and critical consciousness is the one in which teachers and learners find themselves conducting a sort of collaborative search, each from her or his lived situation. . . . Imagining things being otherwise may be a first step toward acting on the belief that they can be changed . . . an imaginative ability is required if the becoming different that learning involves is actually to take place. (pp. 22–23)

The expansive literacy tools of dramatic inquiry, which are available to whoever can imagine their use, can be used to harness the dramatic imagination in order to create classroom spaces where collaborative, dialogic, and critical explorations of diverse cultural worlds become a norm. Classrooms can become communities where people value agency grounded by playful collaborative risk and evolving identities shaped in the dialogic understanding made possible through embracing, performing, and exploring our differences as well as our connections.

We are not naïve about the oppressive demands, felt and feared by teachers, that press to standardize curriculum and box classrooms into spaces closed to the spontaneity, playfulness, and imagination of young people and adults. The teachers we write about in this book have inspired us. We know that even in schools where their work has been under- or unappreciated, spaces may still be created that are open to worlds within and beyond the school walls, and where the vitality and diversity of students with all their challenges and wonder can be celebrated.

SIX

Spoken Word

Performing Poetry and Community

I had become part of an academic community where you
could love school because school did not have to be something
apart from, or in denial of, your own life and multifarious new
lives of your heterogeneous students! School could become, in
fact, a place where students learned about the world and then
resolved, collectively and creatively, to change it!
—June Jordan, *June Jordan's Poetry for the People*, p. 45

On April 4, 2006, before an audience of more than 250 people gathered
in downtown Minneapolis's Westminster Presbyterian Church, 18-year-old
Tish Jones performed her spoken word poem "March for Me" for the first
annual "Go Light the World" event. On this 40th anniversary of Martin
Luther King's assassination, community members gathered to honor not just
the death of this civil rights leader, but his legacy and dream being borne out
in the lives, voices, and poems of a group of dynamic young artists. Thirty
high-school-age spoken-word poets from across the Twin Cities and greater
Minnesota prepared to depart for the Brave New Voices™ International
Youth Poetry Slam Festival in New York City. On this auspicious occasion,
Ms. Jones performed in collaboration with Twin Cities Community Gospel
Choir singer Robert Robinson. Her words were sung and spoken before
family members, fellow poets, teachers, activists, the mayor, city council
members, and ministers. The performance showcased students' literacy
practices beyond the scope and assessment of a traditional classroom.

In the piece "March for Me," Tish uses spoken-word poetry to name
and address multiple forms of oppression and at the same time enact a
positive, activist identity. Tish wrote the poetic piece inspired by a group
of young adult artists and activists setting out to visit college campuses
across the nation where LGBTQ students were not welcome, known as
the "Soul Force Equality Rides." In her sung and spoken poem, she pays

tribute to the individual and the collective lived experiences of her audience members. This African American teen poet describes what it means to encounter oppression and resist being silenced, drawing on the legacy of civil rights leaders who paved the way for changes that benefited all of humanity. She writes:

> And I don't know too many people who have
>   to prove that they're a people
> I mean
> There are exceptions like
> My people
> Who fought for their rights to be equal
> Is this the sequel

Tish makes audible not only her own voice, but also the voices of many who have been told they are not allowed to be free to love and act as they are. She writes and performs her work to celebrate and honor the roots of change—first and foremost by witnessing and testimony. We will return to Tish's poem and its performance later in the chapter, after reviewing what makes spoken-word and related youth forms of cultural expression such a compelling literacy tool.

YOUTH LITERACY PRACTICES EVIDENT IN SPOKEN WORD

Young people's literacy practices are embedded in their everyday critical perception and production of texts that are as rich, varied, and dynamic as students' lives inside and outside the classroom. These texts range from traditional, written forms of literature—their history books, fiction, or science lessons—to those that are visual and aural: the words uttered on the sidewalk, a basketball court, church, or at city hall, and those scribbled or painted on the wall, hanging in a museum, or seen in the human expressions of family members, leaders, strangers, or teachers. From these critical perceptions—that first act of seeing and naming—flow critical questions:

> Who am I? Where am I from? Where am I going? What communities am I connected to and responsible to? What legacies am I heir to? Who has made sacrifices for me? What sacrifices should I make for future generations? What do I do with my indignation? How do I foster love in my community? How can I be an agent of change?

Tish and her peers must also address what role poetry has in these critical reflections and investigations. These questions hone and orient student inquiries, allow students to draw on a range of literacy practices, and give birth to their performance poems.

The students' works have risen organically out of students' actual social contexts and the political realities of their lives. Spoken-word poetry can be an opportunity for students to articulate what fills their hearts, minds, thoughts, and dreams, and provides an opening for teachers to learn from them. When educators learn from students about the conditions that produce inequality, they are better able to participate in collective projects of change and transformation. It begins with the simple, but often overlooked, step of witnessing. The poet describes. The audience listens and responds. In the process, the two are changed; it is a mutual transformation.

Hip-hop scholar and activist Marc Lamont Hill (2009) describes this communal experience of listening and responding as a necessary first step in an individual's and then a community's process of healing. He elaborates on the way hip-hop performance makes visible the invisible through recognizing, acknowledging, and responding to historically inflicted wounds:

> I use the term wounds to refer to those narratives of pain, suffering, and injustice that mediate an individual's understanding and negotiation of the world; healing alludes to those storytelling practices that enabled students to recognize the commonality of their experiences, gain insight into their problems, and access new ideological perspectives; . . . healing refers to an ongoing process of negotiating various personal and ideological struggles in reflective, collective, and productive fashion. (p. 265)

Hill notes that healing is not merely a therapeutic process. It is also an epistemic process that entails gaining access to the truth by viewing the world through new, more enabling ideological perspectives. The youth literacy tool of spoken word not only draws on local experience, but also has roots and affinities with forms of knowledge production in global contexts, such as South Africa. Spoken word presents one avenue for students to affirm that they are not alone in navigating multiple forms of oppression; the art form can foster a community of resistance.

WITNESSING: VOICING EXPERIENCE

"Everyone has a story to tell," said Father Michael Lapsley, director of the Institute for Healing Memories in Cape Town, South Africa. As apartheid activist and chaplain to the African National Congress, Lapsley survived a letter-bombing targeted at him while in exile fighting the White supremacist regime. Returning to South Africa, he participated in the Truth and Reconciliation hearings led by Archbishop Tutu. Like Hill (2009), Father Lapsley (2008) speaks to the ethical dimensions of testimonials and how "hav[ing] your own story reverenced, recognized, acknowledged, and given a moral containment" is a necessary condition for reconciliation and transformation. Father Lapsley also underscores the difference between having knowledge of circumstances and *acknowledging* what occurs or has occurred. Like the poet William Stafford (1998) conveys in "Ritual to Read to Each Other": "I call it cruel and maybe the root of all cruelty to know what occurs but not recognize the fact" (p. 75). When it comes to matters of injustice, there can be no elephants in the room.

One of the affordances of spoken-word poetry as a literacy tool is that it both calls for and creates an audience that has an ethical role of witnessing through voicing to one's experience. The distinction between knowing and acknowledging is an active listening one, "an active reverence," as Lapsley puts it; it is an acknowledgment of what someone has lived through and survived. The poet becomes a medium for society's injustices, and the audience, through responses such as clapping, swaying, and singing (what Hill [2009] refers to as "co-signing"), affirms its truth value.

Tish's poem makes manifest the injustices many have endured, and is intertextually connected to a larger body of poetic narratives authored and performed by teens. Young people address and name topics in their performance poems that are at once endemic to society but also inadequately addressed: racism, homophobia, generational and systemic poverty, physical and sexual abuse, gender inequality, and homelessness, to name a few. The medium also affords an opportunity to celebrate the joys and strengths that come from community and identity.

Like narrative, spoken-word poetry gives students the opportunity to name and describe the circumstances of their lives. Unlike narrative, spoken word is a condensed form of writing and performing—usually 3 to 5 minutes in length for a slam—that employs both literary devices and performance techniques. Along with alliteration, assonance, metaphor, simile, imagery, and rhyme, a poet brings his or her poem to life using repetition, intonation, vocal variety, physical gestures, and body movements. They may sing, rap, or incorporate "beat-boxing" (percussion created with one's mouth and lips) as the work makes its way from the page to the stage. The spoken-word artists make audible their experiences and observations of the world.

This notion of individual and collective voicing differs from the idea of fostering expression of an inner voice reflecting a singular "true self" (Elbow, 2007). Rather than expressing one particular point of view, in performing spoken-word poetry, students are adopting and playing with multiple, dialogic perspectives in a way that reflects Bakhtin's (1981) notion of "double-voicing" different languages in ways that, as June Jordan (1995) notes, privileges the multifarious and captures the blended realities of people's lives.

Critics of spoken word suggest that it is not standard academic English and is too oral. As Anne Dyson (2005) notes, schools have dichotomized the oral and written dimensions of authorship, viewing "speech, not as a solution, but as a major problem for student writers who write like they talk" (p. 153). This view subscribes to narrow and remedial definitions of academic English. As theorists like Brian Street (1995) have noted, there are a plurality of academic literacies that we believe should include culturally inflected "ways with words" (Heath, 1983). It would also be a gross misrepresentation to characterize spoken word as a mere reflection of oral language. It is a sophisticated literary genre that blends written and oral dimensions and formal and informal registers. Spoken-word poets draw from a range of resources that include but are not limited to canonical literature, personal experience, African American language, hip-hop language, and other languages such as Spanish and Tagalog (just listen to the work of Filipino hip-hop artists and activists such as Blue Scholars or Native Guns, or the spoken-word poetry of Mayda del Valle). Anything in youth's multifarious universe is grist for the intellectual and creative mill.

Many students draw on voices from hip-hop culture to constitute identities through performance, dress, languages, attitudes, and stances (Alim, 2006; Chang, 2005, 2007; Mahiri, Ali, Scott, Asmerom, & Ayers, 2008). Mahiri and his colleagues define the hip-hop culture as including:

> (a) DJing (mixing and playing a variety of sound texts), (b) MCing (rapping, mastering ceremony), (c) B-Boying (break-dancing, and now various other dance styles), and (d) graffiti (spray painting colorful words and images, tags and murals, on public spaces) . . . [as well as] "the way you walk, the way you talk, the way you look, the way you communicate. (p. 279)

Rather than police expression of hip-hop culture in the classroom, it is important that teachers be open to learning from the multiple literacies involved in hip-hop practices. For example, Mahiri, Ali, Scott, Asmerom, & Ayers's (2008) analysis of young rap artist 5-Milli found that he continually critiqued the lyrics employed by other rappers, engaging in free styling and rap competitions, writing his own lyrics based on certain beats and genre conventions and on life experiences and current/community events, translating lyrics into performance with attention to speed and delivery style, and recording rap employing different tracks. Students also voice experiences through their physical enactment or embodiment—gestures, movement, facial expression, sound, pitch, pauses, and so forth. Students can read aloud a play or their own work so that they "work out the meanings in remarkable detail and actually feel those meanings in their bodies" (Elbow, 2007, p. 178). Then, by performing the same lines in different ways, students become aware of how differences in the sound of language change the meaning of language. These are sophisticated literacy practices that are consistent with rigorous academic expectation and a quality education. This intellectual and cultural work should be central to schooling.

RETURNING TO TISH'S "MARCH FOR ME"

Tish's poem below embodies many of the features of virtuosic spoken word. The poem begins in song, with a "hook," or refrain, written by Tish, that in this space, on this particular evening, is sung by the gospel performer Robert Robinson. Reflecting on the genesis of the piece as inspired by the young adult activist community working in the tradition of the 1960s Freedom Riders, who are about to set out for the "Soulforce Equality Rides": "The idea was to gather stories from each other and the riders and anyone else we could, and create pieces based off of that . . ." Encouraged by an adult mentor in the community and her peers, Tish read many letters and narratives from members in the LGBTQ movement detailing their experiences coming out and being shunned by family and friends.

> [Robert singing:
> "March for me
> Write for me
> Candle in the night for me
> Hold your head up high for me
> Keep on throwing pride for me
> And I will be
> Okay okay"]
>
> My individual pride keeps telling me not to conform
> But it's hard to stay strong when you are laughed at
> Cast out

Called out
Left out
Ridiculed
Teased
Turned against
Turned on
And hung out to dry
Your whole life long
And I don't know too many people who have to
        prove that they're a people
I mean
There are exceptions like
My people
Who fought for their rights to be equal
Is this the sequel
Will it take a couple more centuries for everyone to
        be seen in the same light
Live with the same rights
Two people in love to get married at every available church site
            Regardless
My individual pride keeps telling me NOT to conform
But it's hard to stay strong
Even though I've got a legacy of leaders 400 years long
And Lady Coretta Scott King sang two freedom songs
One
For the love of my skin
And Two
For the love of him and him
Or
Her and her

[Robert singing:
"March for me
Write for me
Candle in the night for me
Hold your head up high for me
Keep on throwing pride for me
And I will be
Okay okay"]

See
Me and Mine

We mourn all the time
For those that couldn't make it along the journey because
    it's an uphill climb
I
Feel the pain
I
Feel the hurt
I
Sense the tension inside the church

I see you kicked out your house
For wearing all the colors of the rainbow and kissing your spouse
I hear you with your closed mouth
And I know what that's about

You're being shut down
For people fear what they do not understand
but if you believe in a higher power how can you honestly feel
    it okay to judge another man
To cringe at shaking his hand because he's different
This phobia of homosapiens is ridiculous.

[Robert singing:
"When will we understand
That the only way to move forward
Is to love our fellow man
We've lost so many hurt souls
God please show us the way
Fill me up with hope
Walk with me down this road
Cuz I don't know if I can stand
To bear it all alone"]

I lost my best friend to this
Letters from a friend drenched by tears fallen from fear of sin
A suicide note
       And we can never speak again
Tired of living his life
He felt too caged in
Afraid to open his door cuz hate would creep right in
He closed down
And all the love he had slipped out

Now all I have is his whispers in the wind
Pictures of me and him
Memories of way back when
Snapshots of him
Hanging from the basement ceiling
I miss my friend
This is for him

[Robert singing:
"March for me
Write for me
Candle in the night for me
Hold your head up high for me
Keep on throwing pride for me
And I will be
Okay okay"]

It is important to note that the poem was not merely expressive, representing the interior state of an individual, but rather the result of research
(interviews, observations, critical readings) into a collective LGBTQ experience, expressed through double-voicing young people's perspectives
and weaving them into other historical voices. In the opening lines of
the song she wrote, "March for me/Write for me," we hear echoes of the
1960s civil rights movement and the Freedom Rides, which inspired these
Equality Riders.

The Truth and Reconciliation hearings of postapartheid South Africa
were underscored by the concept of *Ubuntu*, described by Archbishop Tutu
(1999): "We are bound up in a delicate network of interdependence because,
as we say in our African idiom, [*Ubuntu* means that] a person is a person
through other persons" (p. 35). In spoken-word poetry venues across the
Unites States, this same concept of *Ubuntu* is at work, through the poets'
performances and their invitations to the audience members to participate.
Tish's poem weaves and blends the narratives of the African American civil
and human rights movement with the struggles for equality of the LGBTQ
community. These links demonstrate human interdependence and mutual
recognition in order to foster solidarity.

The hook of Tish's poem, repeated throughout, serves as a type of anthem. On this particular evening, the sung refrain works as a call-and-re-
sponse between the poet performer and the gospel singer. Leaving the church
space that evening, you could hear people singing these repeated lines. Tish's

melodic phrasing underscores the legacy of the activist and collective identity rooted in resistance, especially when the community claims the anthem
and joins in singing, as occurred during this performance. She identifies the
challenge of remaining strong in identity as she enumerates the many ways
dejection occurs and people are made to feel excluded and "othered": "it's
hard to stay strong when you are laughed at/ Cast out/ Called out/ Left out/
Ridiculed/ Teased/ Turned against/ Turned on/ And hung out to dry/Your
whole life long." Her use of alliteration (C's and T's) and repetition of the
word *out* works in service of the poet's commentary on the experience of
unrelentingly being pushed "out," suggesting an allusion to Audre Lorde's
(2007) *Sister, Outsider* and the LGBTQ process of "coming out."

The poem names and makes visible the wounds experienced daily by
many. Tish describes seeing a person who has been kicked out of his/her
house, and later, a young man who kills himself:

I see you kicked out of your house
For wearing all the colors of the rainbow and kissing your spouse
I hear you with your closed mouth
        And I know what that's about

You're being shut down

I lost my best friend to this
Letters from a friend drenched by tears fallen from fear of sin
A suicide note

By embedding these raw experiences in an anthem of social justice, as
opposed to making an expository statement, the implication is that they can
be the basis for ethical voicing, leading to social action.

SPOKEN-WORD POETRY AND INQUIRY, SPACE, IDENTITY, AND AGENCY

Tish was a member of a performance collective called Teens Rock the Mic.
Formed by a group of teen spoken-word poets from Minneapolis and St.
Paul public high schools, a local youth drop-in center, and with the mentorship of their teachers and adult poets, Teens Rock the Mic produced a
slam series in the winter of 2004 and spring of 2005, qualifying a team for
the Brave New Voices™ International Youth Poetry Slam Festival. With the

success of the "Real Spit" series, as the youth dubbed it, and the subsequent journey to the festival in San Francisco came an outpouring of communal support. The enthusiasm from other poets, mentors, parents, and community leaders led to the continuation of the project.

The Teens Rock the Mic poets began meeting once a week at the Loft Literary Center in Minneapolis. Together, the poets and volunteer mentors created a mission statement that focused on ways to reach out to other young people in the state. They also collaborated with such community agencies as the Peace Foundation in Minneapolis and the Walker Art Center to produce the first "Peace Games" and "Arts Showcase"—bringing young people together across North Minneapolis to participate in athletic competitions and hip-hop performances. The poets produced a final showcase of their performance work, complete with original visual art, which became a multimedia show in the Walker Art Center's McGuire Theater. Through Melissa's arts literacy network in South Africa, the poets hosted three young adult community development workers from abroad. Together, the international group spent time examining critical questions around the intersection of arts and community activism. They contemplated the role that voice and features of poetic narrative can play in making change in their respective communities.

What is perhaps most significant about the Teens Rock the Mic project is that the spoken-word artists were engaging and reaching younger audiences in ways that many teachers and curricula were unable to. They employed what Lee (2007) describes as "cultural modeling" that involves connecting students' cultural experiences with music and language from their own lives to producing poetry as spoken word.

The focus on performance of their poems led to high levels of engagement in which students were suddenly front and center, raising their hands, posing questions, and engaging with the Teens Rock the Mic ensemble. The poets also toured to Duluth for the Race, Culture, and Achievement Gap conference. They were contracted to work with the Duluth, Minnesota, public schools, performing and conducting workshops, and partnered with the Neighborhood Youth Services community center to mentor other young poets as they created their own Open Mic series.

Tish and her peers' performances in Teens Rock the Mic reflect the uses of literacy tools to engage students in critical inquiry, constructing spaces, enacting identity, and establishing agency. The creation of the spoken-word poetry was the result of serious scholarly investigation into people's experiences, which were a source of knowledge and critical insight. The content of Tish's poem was crafted from data she gleaned from a number of qualitative methods as part of an action research inquiry. For example, Tish interviewed friends and community members about their experiences. This inquiry process enabled a collective representation in which histories and struggles intersected and various aspects of identity blended.

In the alternative educational space of Teens Rock the Mic, students were engaged in self-definition. The traditional classroom environment became a public, communal setting where mutual learning took place and the audience expanded beyond teachers and peers. Part of becoming an agent entailed becoming a teacher. The Teens Rock the Mic members developed an educational action plan, took their show on the road, and had a profound influence on young people across the nation. The poets became not only performers, but facilitators of critical discourse and inquiry based on the art of their craft.

USING SPOKEN-WORD POETRY IN THE CLASSROOM

Educators are uniquely positioned to advocate for spoken word in the classroom and provide a space for nurturing the poetic brilliance of future generations. In using spoken word in the classroom, teachers need to adopt a stance of humility by being willing to learn from their students. With that spirit in mind, we offer the following recommendations for educators who are interested and committed to incorporating spoken-word poetry in the classroom.

Attend an Open Mic or Teen Poetry Slam

Students and teachers need to experience the power of spoken word firsthand by going to open mic or teen poetry slams in local coffee shops, bookstores, and nightclubs. They can also tune into HBO's *Russell Simmons Presents Brave New Voices* (their Web site contains extensive resources), and the Nuyorican Poets Café Web page (http://www.nuyorican.org), or view David Yanofsky's one-hour video documentary, *Poetic License* (http://www.itvs.org/poeticlicense/index.html). *Urban Youth Poets: Quest for the Voice*, available on YouTube, is one video documentary, among many, capturing youth performances. Teachers can also read June Jordan's (1995) *June Jordan's Poetry for the People: A Revolutionary Blueprint*, Maisha Fisher's (2007) *Writing in Rhythm: Spoken-Word Poetry in Urban Classrooms*, Jen Weiss and Scott Herndon's (2001) *Brave New Voices: The Youth Speaks Guide to Teaching Spoken-Word Poetry*, or the young adult fiction novel *Bronx Masquerade* by Nikki Grimes (2003), about a high school teacher who institutes an open mic in the classroom.

Invite Spoken-Word Artists Into the Classroom

It is also useful to have spoken-word artists from the community come into classrooms; teachers can also bring in recordings of artists' live performances. This will ground the community of learners in a common experience of the art form and provide an entrée into their collective unpacking of the work, making visible its affordances. Following a live performance of spoken-word poets, students can ask, "What do you notice?" "What did you hear?" They can also address, using the Critical Response Protocol, issues and themes of the poet's work.

Following a Teens Rock the Mic performance, for example, in a school's auditorium or community space, Melissa, one of the mentors, and/or one of the teen poets would facilitate a discussion of the work using the Critical Response Protocol, posing questions such as "What did you notice or feel in responding to spoken word?," "What connections did you make?," and "Why spoken word?" Through this facilitated inquiry process, students, teachers, staff, and any present community leaders would be able to echo back lines of the teen poetry, acknowledging what stood out to them.

Establish a Spoken-Word Residency:
Reflecting on Language, Sound, and Literary Devices

Working with a spoken-word artist in the classroom, teachers and students can confidently write, workshop, and rehearse their own original poems. Just as they would in studying literature, students can describe the uses of language, sound, and literary devices, by, as Maisha Fisher (2005) notes, making the "process of being or becoming literate as visible as possible" (p. 97). Students can identify those specific uses of language that resonate with them, leading to the creation of a list of what makes good spoken-word poetry.

In Teens Rock the Mic Spoken-Word Poetry residencies, for example, Melissa would partner with a teen spoken-word artist and co-facilitate such list creations with a classroom of learners. On a large sheet of paper students wrote responses to the questions, "What makes a good poem?" and "What do good performers do?" Following the performance of a poem, the students and teacher would identify what they saw or heard at work in the performed poem, leading to identification of instances of alliteration, assonance, rhyme, metaphor, simile, and repetition. These reflections on technique underscore the intellectual rigor and academic relevance of spoken word.

Spoken-word artists in the classroom can also serve as mentors to assist students, demonstrating ways to become involved in local spoken-word performance groups, what Maisha Fisher (2005) describes as "participatory literacy communities" (p. 116). These artists can model practices while students are writing, rehearsing, and performing so that students can immediately apply these techniques to their own performances. These communities can also provide "a neutral space where students were encouraged to maintain a nonjudgmental attitude toward their peers [through] a 'culture of listening' and valuing words" (Fisher, 2005, p. 127).

Recognize Students' Initial Apprehension About Performing Publicly

Because students may be apprehensive about publicly reading aloud their work to their peers, it is important to directly address these fears. In describing one community, Korina Jocson (2005) noted that mentors who helped students practice their performances shared their own fears about public speaking by performing:

> different scenarios such as reading too fast or too slowly, reading while chewing gum, reading behind a piece of paper or book, reading while fidgeting or playing with one's hair, among others. [The mentors] reminded students what the most important aspect in the whole public reading experience was—to own their words, deliver them with an air of confidence, and have fun with them. (p. 145)

Produce a Slam for the School or Community

Teachers can collaborate with students, given their own experiences, to create a poetry slam for the school or community. Students can discuss what makes a good slam or how they will score (judge) poems in order to develop plans related to issues of quality, audience, voice, community, and production standards, as well as questions such as, "How do we grade art? What score do you place on someone's life story or poetic experience?" This can lead to co-creating a rubric for a successful slam, fleshing out and naming what makes good poetry and what makes good performance. The student producers can create scoring ballots, and in the process bring the slam to fruition.

In his book *Roc the Mic Right*, sociolinguist Samy Alim (2006) asks the invaluable question, "At what price will we continue to ignore the extraordinary linguistic, literary and literacy skills of this generation of young Black Americans?" (p. 3). Addressing Tish and Teens Roc the Mic, Minneapolis

City Councilman Don Samuels (2006) gives a sense of what would be gained from harnessing the profound knowledge and talents of contemporary youth.

> You demonstrate the courage of honest speech. You speak of thoughts many of us shy away from. Your spoken words often break debilitating taboos. Your spoken words defy the risks of vulnerability. Some things are too painful for us to express. . . . Through your spoken words you help liberate us from all the unarticulated anxieties. And from your speech, full of seduction of poetry and art, we cannot turn away. You have held us captive. . . . [You] ask the questions that begin great dialogues. [You] pose the kind of dilemmas that begin theological developments.

This response represents the power of spoken-word poetry performances to enable students to engage in personal and collective self-definition (Wissman, 2009). As the councilman recognizes, these voices not only need to be heard, they should influence and inform policy to bring about systemic changes.

SEVEN

Digital Literacies

Virtually Connecting and Collaboratively Building Knowledge

In her fall 2008 College Writing course for 12th graders at a high school located in suburban Minneapolis, Elizabeth Boeser was not satisfied with her students' engagement in writing essays. This led her to develop an online role-play for her classes around the topic of the school's Internet policies. The students were agitated that administrators in a neighboring high school suspended students for violating athletic rules governing alcohol use based on Facebook photos. The students were also upset about the fact that in conducting research on certain topics in their own school, for example, gun control, they would find that certain sites such as that of the National Rifle Association would be blocked.

To prepare for this role-play, Elizabeth had students read the school's current Internet policies regarding rationales for blocking certain sites, which the students found to be quite vague. She assigned roles representing a range of competing pro–con perspectives on these issues, including those of administrators, teachers, students, parents, librarians, businesspeople, school board members, and technology coordinators. Students created avatars and posted their arguments using a Ning social networking site, a digital literacy tool similar to Facebook or MySpace that allows students to create profiles and to participate in a discussion forum. Students debated the issue as to whether sites should be blocked in their school, as well as whether administrators have the right to access their Facebook pages.

In creating online roles, students often assumed positions contrary to their own beliefs, and subsequently considered alternative arguments for blocking or not blocking sites. In adopting the role of an outspoken student opponent of blocking sites, Ali Christensen noted that:

> I created the character Judith Rosario as something of a foil to
> myself. She is outspoken, loud, and more than a little opinionated.
> She believes in total and uninhibited free speech that should
> not and cannot be restricted. I began the role-play believing that

administration's monitoring of student access was a good idea, but my opinions changed a little as time progressed. As I continued to write as Judith, and research the topic more carefully, I came to see how a person could come to feel so strongly about privacy in the academic setting.

Elizabeth made it clear to the students that, based on their participation in the online role-play, they would be proposing changes in the school's Internet policies to the school's administration. Knowing that they had the agency to do so served to motivate the students to develop convincing arguments. As Mike Kujak, another student, noted about these policies:

> Not only does the [school] handbook set unclear rules or punishment for offenders, but it also states that the administration does not support any of the sites that are blocked. Half of the sites that are blocked are done not because of content but guilt by association.
>
> We have a chance to change something that will continually make a difference. We can stand up for ourselves and show that we don't need protection from the big bad world anymore. We can put forward our own beliefs and represent ourselves for a change. Finally, we can sit down with the school board and set some clear rules for students to follow, and then inform the students on the rules so that they know they are breaking them.

Students wrote persuasive essays, based on their own and others' arguments formulated during the role-play, that served as material for arguing their position to the school's technology coordinator, who had the authority to unblock sites.

The online forum provided students with opportunities to formulate arguments over an extended period of time during and after class. In creating their bios and avatars on the Ning site, they were constructing a virtual identity and stance that shaped their positions consistent with certain beliefs and discourses. For example, some students assuming administrator and parent roles adopted a discourse of control and protection, arguing that students should not be exposed to sites that might promote undesirable behavior. In contrast, some students in student roles argued that being able to access and negotiate complex and controversial information is a necessary component of educating for democratic citizenship. In the forum, students exposed to a wide range of different pro and con positions provided counterargument comments and linked to articles and materials bolstering their arguments, for example, information about court cases related to free speech and censorship.

The collected posts from the role-play served as useful prewriting material for students in composing essays. Students reviewed their own and others' posts and drew on competing arguments to craft their own positions on the problems of not having access to blocked sites for educational purposes. When the students presented their arguments to the school's technology coordinator, the coordinator unblocked sites, including allowing teachers access to YouTube in their classes. Through their use of collaborative arguments using a digital literacy tool, students gained a sense of agency to make changes in their school (Beach & Doerr-Stevens, 2009).

USING DIGITAL LITERACY TOOLS IN 21ST-CENTURY CLASSROOMS

Elizabeth's students' use of the Ning discussion forum demonstrates how digital literacy tools—blogs, wikis, Twitter, social networking sites, digital storytelling—enable students to critically investigate an issue that concerns them (Beach, Anson, Kastman-Breuch, & Swiss, 2008; Richardson, 2009) (for links to information on these digital literacy tools, see http://digitalwriting.pbworks .com, and links on the book's wiki site, http://literacytooluses.pbworks.com). Students in the online role-play created virtual identities/avatars as personas designed to enhance their arguments. Both during and after school they also shared and responded to one another's posts, which could be read by multiple audiences. And to support their positions, they could readily search for and link to material that served as valuable preparation for writing essays and making their case to the technology coordinator.

In the process, they were acquiring digital literacies. As evident in the use of Twitter and cell phones to broadcast the details of the 2009 Iranian election to the world, as well as the use of online social networking in the 2008 Obama campaign, young people use digital literacy tools to become change agents; as citizen researchers, activists, and journalists, their bottom-up communications challenge the top-down control of information by traditional mainstream media. Because these tools allow for instant sharing of engaging, multimodal information, they can be used to foster collaborative critical inquiry and political activity.

It is often the case that students learn to use digital literacy tools outside of schools, as evident in their use of social networking sites, blogs, or Twitter in a networked, participatory culture (Lenhart, Arafeh, Smith, & Macgill, 2008). Rather than limit the use of such tools in schools, it is essential that teachers build on and add their own critical dimension to these media, as did Elizabeth in fostering use of argumentative writing using the Ning.

While some teachers may resist incorporation of digital literacies given pressure to prepare for print-based reading and writing assessments and other teachers may replace print with digital literacies, Kevin Leander (2009) posits the need for a "parallel pedagogy" approach that integrates both print and digital literacies and that re-mediates traditional print-based generic forms. For example, students may combine print memoir pieces with digital stories to reflect on how "the old is absorbed and routinely transformed into new forms" (p. 161).

CONSTRUCTING ONLINE IDENTITIES

Digital literacy tools also serve to foster engagement with participation in on-line communities in which students acquire identities and a sense of agency. Through enacting online personas on Facebook, MySpace, or Twitter, students are constructing identities as members of online communities, or what danah boyd (2006) defines as "networked publics" (p. 9). These online communities have the properties of "persistence" (communication is recorded and stored), "searchability" (people can readily locate one another and information), "replicability" (material can be copied and moved), and "invisible audiences" (it is difficult to identify one's potential audiences) (p. 9). Boyd (2006) explains that "bloggers also speak about their blogs being their online identity, their digital representation . . . the blog gives them a locatable voice and identity in the digital world . . . bloggers view their blogs as them" (p. 12).

Learning to engage in online interaction involves what Michael Wesch (2009) describes as acquiring "subjectivities: ways of approaching, under-standing, and interacting with the world" (p. 3) through creating online "environments in which the practices and perspectives are nourished, en-couraged, or inspired (and therefore continually practiced)" (p. 3). For ex-ample, in his Introduction to Cultural Anthropology course at Kansas State University, Wesch created an online World Simulation that involves students in becoming experts in the culture of a specific region of the world, using a wiki to share information and digital videos to portray that information. Students then extract notions of what it means to operate in different cultures, including how these cultures may or may not be connected.

Students also use digital literacy tools to communicate with audiences outside the classroom, where they are exposed to alternative perspectives and ideas that challenge status-quo thinking. For example, students can communicate with students in other schools on sites such as Youth Voices (http://youthvoices.net/elgg) or online virtual versions of texts on the Literary Worlds site (http://www.literaryworlds.org) (Rozema & Webb, 2008). On the Literary Worlds site, students can engage in synchronous chat about frequently taught texts such as *Brave New World*, *Of Mice and Men*, *The Great Gatsby*, and *1984*. By engaging in virtual worlds in the same way that they participate in game worlds, students create their own versions of characters and settings in the texts.

ACQUIRING DIGITAL LITERACIES

Through their use of digital literacy tools, students acquire four important digital literacies: multimodality, hyperlinking, connectivity, and collaboration.

Multimodality

Multimodality means combining or remixing text, images, video, and audio to create digital productions (Kress, 2003). In creating digital storytelling or poetry, students combine a number of different modes, such as print text, audio, images, and video. Because these texts are digital, students can capture, combine, and remix them to share with peers (Rozema & Webb, 2008). For example, in working with his eighth-grade students at West Junior High School, Hopkins, Minnesota, Brent Eckoff describes how he uses the Comic Life (http://plasq.com/comiclife) program as students create comic book interpretations of stories:

> As a prewriting exercise to the first "Comic Life" project, I had students do a rough storyboard of what they planned to create. This involved a six cell, blank comic strip in which they drew rough sketches and included text below each sketch to explain which part of the story they were depicting. They learned quickly that to find images that suit their needs would require various combinations of words and phrases due to the strange tags people tend to place on their photos. They also learned creative ways to use Comic Life to alter images to make them suit their purposes. In addition to altering photos, the limitations Flickr placed on their searches forced them to get more creative with the text they chose to include. Some of the speech bubbles and text boxes they wrote were both surprising, and innovative. The students then exported the Comic Life presentations as Quicktime files, uploaded them to YouTube, and then embedded them on the class wiki (http://eckhoffla .pbwiki.com).

My favorite part about incorporating all of these new digital tools into my classroom is not the new modes of expression or the innovative ideas it brings out in my students; it is the 100% engagement.

Another useful digital literacy tool for combining audio and visual modes is VoiceThread (http://voicethread.com), which can be used to add audio commentary to a photo slide show. For example, in Delainia Haug's Media Studies course, as part of the DigMe program at Roosevelt High School, Minneapolis, Minnesota, described in the Introduction, students created VoiceThread commentaries about their experiences in coping with challenges in their lives. For example, in Delainia's class, Maria Schaeffer and Leosha Bellfield created a VoiceThread production based on research about issues with teen pregnancy (http://voicethread.com/share/296605/). They added commentary to images of teen mothers with their babies such as the following:

Some may not want their babies. Some may want their babies for idealized and unrealistic reasons. Others may feel the child as an achievement and not recognize the serious responsibility a child comes with. Some may keep a child to please another family member. Depression is also common because they are overrun by guilt and fears about the future and just want someone to love.

In their VoiceThread presentation, students included an image of an empty classroom desk to represent the idea of a teen parent not attending school. Their presentation went beyond moralizing: It pointed to the need for society to better support young mothers in realizing their educational ambitions. The use of multimodality also helped convey the complexity and simultaneity of experience that does not fall into simple genrelike categories such as tragedy or joyousness. When various modes such as voice and images are presented in concert, the author/designers are better able to communicate complex emotions associated with becoming a new parent.

Learning to create multimodal digital texts requires the ability to know how to combine, mesh, or remix images, video, audio, and text in ways that engage audiences, something we discuss in more detail in Chapter 9. For example, in creating digital storytelling texts, students need to know how to use images to create narrative conflicts. Students also need a semiotic sense of how certain images resonate with audiences based on popular culture meanings, for example, how an empty chair conveys symbolic meanings about a student not attending school.

In creating multimodal texts, students may be using digital copyrighted material. Because they are reworking or transforming copyrighted texts, this "transformative" use for their own critical and pedagogical purposes of revising, interpreting, critiquing, and parodying material falls under the legal doctrine of "fair use" of such texts, with proper attribution of the original text. For a description of idea of the transformational fair use of digital media related to the fair use doctrine (Center for Social Media, 2008), see http://www .centerforsocialmedia.org/resources/publications/fair_use_in_online_video/.

Hyperlinking

In composing digital media, as students create hyperlinks between texts, they are involved in the digital literacy of knowing how to understand and employ intertextual connections between different ideas (Bernstein & Greco, 2009). For example, students can create hypertext autobiographical essays in which they forge links between aspects of their lives and historical events, local places, or popular culture topics. They may also study media representations of certain topics by finding images on Flickr or videos on YouTube and then combining these with voiceover text on VoiceThread. In creating their VoiceThread production on teen pregnancy, Maria and Leosha selected images such as the empty classroom chair because they believed that it would dramatize the issue of gender inequality with respect to educational access, especially for young mothers. This suggests the importance of defining one's purpose for using a hyperlink or connection to an image. Students also need to envision how audiences may process texts given those audiences' own purposes. In order to self-assess and reflect, they could pose the following questions:

- What do you want your audiences to learn from your text? How does that determine the links or connections you are using?
- What may be some purposes audiences bring to your text—what do they want to find or learn in reading your text?
- What cues, icons, prompts, or directions will you use to help audiences use the links or connections to find what they are looking for or learn certain things?

Students also use links to others' ideas to develop their own line of thinking. Joseph Harris (2006) describes this linking as "forwarding" others' ideas and positions. This forwarding also involves "borrowing: What you draw on, terms or ideas from other writers to use in thinking through your subject" (p. 39) and "authorizing: When you invoke the expertise or status of another writer to support your thinking" (p. 39). By linking to others' ideas, students are also ideally engaged in "extending: When you put your own spin on the terms of concepts that you take from other texts" (p. 39). For example, in Meredith Aby's 12th-grade AP U.S. Government class at Jefferson High School, Bloomington, Minnesota, students created blog posts about their perceptions of the 2008 presidential campaign (http://2008presidentialrace-meredith.blogspot.com). In their posts, students drew heavily on one anothers' posts as well as on a range of different news and blog sites. One student, Jessica Lieb, took issue with her peer's argument that John McCain's vice presidential candidate, Sarah Palin, was not a liability for the Republican campaign:

> I have to disagree with AJ's claim that Sarah Palin didn't hurt the McCain campaign. I also disagree with people's argument that while her celebrity status towards the end of the race hindered his campaign, she was a positive asset at the beginning because of her relatable status. I disagree with this claim because I believe that McCain's selection of her as his running mate symbolized his loss of the chance to become our next president. Palin summarized all of the things McCain should not have played up in his election. Americans did not want another "old maverick" in the White House. . . . The choice of Sarah Palin as his running mate symbolized John McCain's movement towards ambiguity and empty promises, which was the last thing Americans wanted to hear with our economic crises.

In her post, Jessica is disagreeing with another student's position on John McCain's selection of Sarah Palin as his vice-presidential nominee. To do so, she drew on a number of links that she cites: 1) http://www.washington post.com/wp-dyn/content/article/2008/10/27/AR2008102702406.htm, 2) http://www.politico.com/news/stories/0908/13062.html, and 3) http://themoderatevoice.com/politics/sarah-palin/24121/did-sarah-palin-lose-the-election-for-mccain/. She is borrowing ideas from these links and extending those facts to develop her own position as to why McCain's selection of Sarah Palin reflected his own "ambiguity and empty promises," forwarding this material to generate and support her own opinion.

Connectivity

Digital literacy also involves connectivity—the ability to employ digital communication tools to socially connect and network with others. Through making connections, students build personal learning networks (PLNs) for creating social relationships and acquiring knowledge. Learning to network with others has become as essential literacy tool in the knowledge economy; given the short-term, transient nature of employment, people need to know how to promote themselves through networking.

The theory of connectivism suggests that learning revolves around knowing how to use digital literacy tools to create and use networks to acquire information and build social relationships (Downes, 2007; Siemens, 2008). Because information is readily available online and through the media, students now need to know not only where or from whom to access that information but also how to critically synthesize it to achieve new knowledge and understandings. And, given the vast amount of information available, students also need to be able to search for, filter, and adjudicate the relevance, validity, and currency of information consistent with their needs. Teachers can model their own use of search strategies by making explicit their decision-making, for example, identifying their purposes and whether search results fulfill those purposes. Students can also use tools such as the Critical Web Reader (http://cwr.indiana.edu) to analyze sites, post inquiry questions, assess the relevancy of information to those questions, and critically analyze the biases operating on sites.

Students also use digital literacy tools to build social connections with other students, as evident in the popularity of texting and social networking sites. Teachers can have their classes connect with each other to exchange ideas. In one instance, as mentioned in Chapter 2, students in Melissa's 10th-grade class at North High School were studying Zora Neale Hurston's (1937/1991) *Their Eyes Were Watching God*. As part of their study, they exchanged e-mail responses with Joy Hanson's 10th-grade students at a suburban Minneapolis high school. In their planning, Melissa and Joy were curious about what would happen as these quite different groups of students responded to issues of race, class, and gender difference.

To begin, they asked students to complete pre-unit survey questions related to their preconceptions of suburban and urban students. The North High students then created four representations of urban female and male students, as well as depictions of the suburban students. Students at the suburban school created images of students in both schools. They then created video introductions of their classes to exchange, followed by ongoing cross-school e-mail exchanges with partners of their responses to the novel. Students discussed what fueled their preconceived images of urban and suburban students, particularly in terms of how media representations portray urban and suburban worlds as completely distinct.

Following this exchange, students met face-to-face, where they dis-covered that their counterparts were experiencing similar interests and challenges in ways that defied their stereotypes about each other. They recognized that they had similar responses; they had shared insights ac-quired through their online communication that would never have oc-curred in their segregated worlds. They were using digital literacy tools to break down borders and barriers, leading to cross-cultural understand-ing (for another example, see the PICCLE Moodle courses [http://piccle .ed.psu.edu] offered in several countries, designed to promote cross-cul-tural understanding).

Students can also foster connections with peers on sites such as Youth Voices (http://youthvoices.net) to engage in collaborative critical inquiry projects. Paul Allison (2009) notes how his students shared critical inquiry questions with others on Youth Voices:

> I ask my students to find a question or a set of questions that they develop in their own speculative writing, and eventually they do online research about their questions, connecting with others who have published on the Internet, and critically interpreting the welter of information available to them there. Students grow their blogs over a semester of working with other students and teachers who share their social network, Youth Voices. (p. 98)

He also poses questions for his students to consider in their blogging:

- What are you passionate about and how do these interests fit with other students' big questions?
- What voices or sources of information do you think are important to include in your search for answers?
- How do you become an effective online networker and get people with shared interests to value your voice online?
- How can you use our social networks as personal learning sites that lead to social action? (p. 110)

Students can use audio digital literacy tools to communicate with one another, particularly given the popularity of cell phones and podcasts on iPods and other audio listening devices. Given the ubiquity of cell phone use, students continually connect with each other through texting and voice mail. In her 12th-grade International Baccalaureate English course at Champlin Park High School, Champlin, Minnesota, Linda Mork employed cell phones as a digital literacy tool to create podcasts of oral commentaries about the students' literature reading. Students recorded their commentaries on their cell phones using Gcast.

Setting up this assignment could not have been easier. During class, I had each student register for a free account at Gcast and create a personal podcast "channel." Because each channel can host many podcasts, students only had to do this step once. Several times throughout the course, students were assigned to call in and record their commentaries. Working in teams of three or four, students regularly visited their teammates' channels, listened to each other's commentaries, and wrote peer evaluations which were distributed and discussed in class. To make finding their teammates' channels easier, I had students create links to their URLs on a class wiki page.

Students found Gcast easy, helpful, and enjoyable. Many commented on how much they looked forward to posting a new podcast and admitted to listening to other students' channels out of curiosity and "just for fun." I believe this authentic audience raised the level of concern and encouraged students to work on improving their commentaries much more than a teacher-only or even small-group audience would have. Many students also stated that this practice greatly reduced their anxiety about the assessment; I can report significant improvement in students' performances.

In addition to recording their responses to texts, students could also record commentaries about lectures, field trips, or school/community events, including interviews with participants.

One advantage of using cell phones is that students who do not have access to computers in their homes are more likely to have access to cell phones. If students do not have access to a cell phone, they can also record podcasts on computers using Garageband (on Macs) or Audacity (http://audacity.source-forge.net/). For some tutorials created by Richard and Pete McCauley on using these podcasting tools, see http://digitalwriting.pbworks.com/McCauley+and+Beach:+Tutorials+on+Creating+Podcasts.

Collaboration

A fourth aspect of digital literacy is the ability to use digital literacy tools such as wikis to engage in collaboration. Wikis—Web sites that multiple users can add to and revise—can be created using tools such as PBWorks (http://pbworks.com), Wikispaces (http://www.wikispaces.com), or Wetpaint (http://www.wetpaint.com) that allow both teachers and students to write and share information (Beach, Anson, Kastman-Breuch, & Swiss, 2009; Richardson, 2009). Students may also use Google Docs (http://docs.google.com) for collaborative writing.

In his high school literature class, Scott Wertsch used wikis to create literature circle discussions of books, with each literature circle sharing their responses on the wiki (http://wertsch.pbworks.com/Book+Club+Wiki+Pages). Students in each literature circle added their own analysis of the novel they were reading so that students were sharing responses both in face-to-face discussions and online. For her 12th grade AP Literature class, Molly Melton used a wiki as a repository of information around topics such as literary terms, critical lenses, texts read, literary analysis, and interpretations (http://molliwog .pbwiki.com). For example, she notes that the "texts" page serves:

> as a place to post musings, observations, questions, images, analysis and other resources corresponding to each piece. Each student, or a pair of students, could be assigned to be the main "author(s)" of the wiki page for one text. Images could be found on Flickr that relate to the content, symbols, or themes of the piece and posted on the wiki.

In another collaborative project, Jennifer Budenski, who teaches at an off-campus alternative program in Hopkins, Minnesota, decided to have her students design a Web site for their school—something it previously lacked— using Google Sites (http://sites.google.com/site/ocphapproject/Home), a free tool for creating Web pages. The students broke up into groups to focus on different aspects of the Web site. Jennifer describes the experience of one student, Demetrius:

> Demetrius decided to compose a Heroes and Role Models page. First, he interviewed fellow students about their personal heroes. Next, he searched for images, asking along the way who some of them were, occasionally diverting to google them. Finally, he attempted to post them on his subpage.
>
> On the last day of the project, Demetrius opened his subpage to discover that another student had attempted to write a brief introduction naming what the chosen heroes and role models shared in common. Finding this small contribution on his page seemed to motivate him for a final effort. Also on this day, another student and I discovered through trial and error over a few days how to insert a Picasa [a Google photo-hosting site] slide show on a subpage. Demetrius discovered his solution. Rather than struggling to manipulate the images on his page, we placed them in a slide show.
>
> I loved the experimentation and frustration of the recursive thinking and composing, and the clarifying effect both of collaborative writing and translation of information from verbal to visual text. We

didn't know what our composition would look like or read like until it was finished. All students learned how a multimodal composition could communicate more clearly than verbal text in this situation.

The outcome that students nearly unanimously appreciated was collaboration. While they had plenty of criticism for other aspects of the unit (one student called it "chaos"), all but three students said they felt like they were all working together on this project.

Over the 20 days of our unit, assessment became a matter of triage. What problem can we solve today, and who's going to be in charge of working on it? Who can help? If we all worked toward making progress on the site, we all earned our participation credit for the day. We also stopped at the midpoint and at the end to view the site as a whole to evaluate it, reassessing our to-do lists. In the end, students received academic points for completing their individual projects and writing feedback at the midpoint and end of the project. They will share an academic grade for the site as a whole.

One advantage of using these digital literacy tools is that rather than having to work together in the same face-to-face setting, students can contribute and revise their writing from different places and times, further enhancing the ease of collaboration. By using digital literacy tools, students learn to work together with others by contributing their own particular knowledge and expertise, collaboration essential for participating in the workplace and society. They can recognize how they may generate higher-quality work by working together than working alone.

In using these digital literacy tools to connect with and collaborate with others, students acquire a sense of the power of collective action, where the sum of everyone's contribution is greater than the isolated parts; this awareness challenges traditional academic ideologies of individual expertise and authorship. They also learn to define their own identities as digital producers in terms of their particular expertise or ability in contributing to collaborative projects. And they learn to assess the effectiveness and appeal of their digital texts, leading them to continually improve in their uses of digital literacies.

EIGHT

Reflective Writing

Nurturing Exploration of Our Lives

In this chapter, we describe the reflective writing tools of freewriting, journal writing, fieldnotes, and mapping (Anson & Beach, 1995; Brannon, Griffin, Haag, Iannone, Urbanski, & Woodward, 2008). We define reflective writing as a vehicle for ongoing student investigation, discovery, and critical inquiry to foster development of unfolding ideas versus a mere representation of already preformulated ideas.

Having to write down their thoughts serves to focus students' attention in a sustained, systematic manner; students may develop their thinking about a topic or experience beyond the superficial. Because these tools involve more process-oriented and spontaneous approaches than the drive for a final product in traditional essay writing, students are likely to more freely shape thoughts and take risks.

Documenting thoughts in writing also provides students with a record for ongoing review and reflection. For example, students may use note-taking to formulate responses to a reading or lecture. Or, at the beginning of class, they may engage in a 5-minute freewrite about a topic in order to prepare for a discussion where they draw on their freewrites to share perspectives. Then, at the end of class, they conduct another 5-minute freewrite to reflect on how their ideas may have evolved.

The use of writing tools to foster reflection was evident in a service-learning social studies course called "JagCorps," taught by Aaron Schram at Jefferson High School, Bloomington, Minnesota. The 12th-grade students volunteered in elementary schools, Habitat for Humanity, food pantries, the Goodwill, Salvation Army, and other sites on Tuesday through Thursday. On Monday and Friday they planned, worked on fund-raising efforts, and shared reflections about their experiences.

The goals of the class were, as defined by Schram, to help students cultivate their own understandings of "what it means to be an active, responsible citizen; the concepts of and the connection between civic work and the common good; and important social issues that influence society and the community." These were related to the idea "that to be a part of something larger than yourself is to gain meaning and purpose in life." Through working with people in various sites, students hoped to improve lives and, in doing so, enhanced their own sense of agency as active citizens. Students used weekly journal entries to reflect on how their experiences enhanced their learning, as well as instances in which they were frustrated about challenges they encountered at their sites. Emily Culhane wrote the following about her experience working in an elementary school program for autistic children:

> My first impressions from the school were that it was a place where they want to help every child. They have three different rooms dedicated to autism; the teachers can use their own techniques to help the kids learn better.
>
> Volunteering at the school has changed my perspective. It really shows you how patient and calm the teachers are in order to work with the kids. It also shows how every child is unique. Some kids you can tell have autism while others even after volunteering with them I never would've guessed they have autism.
>
> The most challenging part of the experience is probably just learning how to deal with the kids in certain situations. I don't know their routines and what is expected of them so I kind of just play with them. I think once I know what they are capable of doing and what they're expected to do and what's norm, I'll feel more comfortable.

Emily uses her writing to define and develop her ideas about how to best work with autistic students. For example, she recognizes that she needs to treat each student as unique. While she might have realized this in conversations with her peers, writing helped her develop emerging understandings in a focused and sustained manner.

FEATURES OF REFLECTIVE WRITING TOOLS

It is useful to model various features of reflective writing tools by describing how they achieve the purposes of fostering reflective learning.

Spontaneous Expression of Ideas

A key aspect of reflective writing is its spontaneity; students can write down their thoughts without editing or censoring over concern for audiences (Elbow, 1973). Getting their thoughts down on paper as quickly as possible serves to alleviate some of the apprehension students have about writing, particularly students who are concerned about making errors or believe they need to edit their writing for an audience. Not being overly concerned about structuring or editing means that students focus on voicing their feelings, opinions, ideas, and reflections.

A Tentative and Exploratory Stance

With reflective writing, students adopt a tentative, exploratory stance in which they entertain hypothetical, "passing theories" (Kent, 1993), hunches, or competing perspectives. Rather than being concerned about generating a definitive, final statement of their ideas, they use writing to explore different or contradictory perspectives on those ideas; this process opens them to interrogating their own positions or entertaining competing positions. Students are not under pressure to convince an audience but, rather, are simply trying out or testing possibilities.

Generating One's Own Language and Ideas

In using reflective writing, for example, note-taking, students are going beyond simply recording or quoting others' ideas from a book or lecture by translating ideas into their own language. In doing so, they internalize and contextualize using their own schema and purposes. And by defining particular writing purposes based on critical inquiry questions, students will select the information most relevant to addressing their concerns.

Conversational Interaction with Others

Because many students prefer to talk out their ideas with others rather than work alone, students can use informal writing as a tool for co-constructing their thoughts through dialogue–journal exchanges, blogging/Twittering, instant messaging, or online chat. Engaging in conversation with others provides students with different perspectives or challenges and a need to extend or reformulate their ideas.

Visual Representations Through Drawing or Mapping of Ideas

Reflective writing tools may also include creating visual representations of ideas through drawing or mapping. Visual images not only illustrate students' writing, but may also foster further analysis. For example, creating a map of the connections between different characters in a novel may inspire students to write new interpretations of characters' relationships.

FREEWRITING

Freewriting consists of spontaneously recording one's thoughts without being overly concerned for organization or editing, as when writing for an audience (Elbow, 1973). One purpose of freewriting is to foster fluency or comfort in expressing one's ideas; students gain confidence in their use of writing to formulate their ideas and in their ability to focus their thoughts on a particular topic or idea in a sustained, consistent manner.

To foster students' oral composing, rather than have them write, they can dictate their thoughts to a peer, a digital recorder, a computer webcam microphone, or speech-to-text dictating software such as Dragon NaturallySpeaking (Windows only), IBM ViaVoice (Windows and Mac), or iListen (Mac); Windows 7 and Windows Vista include Windows Speech Recognition.

Teachers can ask all students to freewrite for 5 to 7 minutes at the beginning of class about the same issue, topic, or question, or about those that small groups may be addressing. For example, if the class is discussing how characters have and use power in a novel, students could freewrite about their own experiences coping with similar power differences in their relationships. Students can always extend their initial freewriting by taking a certain word, phrase, or idea from their initial freewriting and then do another freewrite about that word, phrase, or idea, what Peter Elbow (1973) describes as "looping" from one freewrite to the next.

Freewriting can also be used for discussion-starters in small or large groups. Teachers can pull out quotes from students' writing to read aloud anonymously or to share on a class projector. To foster his students' critical inquiry into issues of race in their class discussions in his 12th-grade literature class in a St. Paul, Minnesota, high school, Daryl Parks (Beach, Haertling-Thein, & Parks, 2008) selected multiple quotes from students' journals and handed them out as a list. He invited students to circle the three quotes they perceived to be the most controversial, which were then used as a platform for critical dialogue. For example, one quote was, "White people as a group enjoy an easier life than anybody else in the country" (pp. 132–133). These freewrites provoked debates about issues of white privilege and portrayals of institutional racism in multicultural literature.

Students also used freewriting at the end of a class to reflect on what they learned that day and how they could apply what they learned to their homework or a long-term project. At the end of a discussion, Parks's students completed a freewrite reflection about instances of White privilege that they experienced in their everyday lives.

NOTE-TAKING

A related reflective writing tool is note-taking for recording thoughts and reactions to readings, presentations, Web sites, or experiences. As previously noted, a primary purpose for using note-taking is not only to record information, but also to translate and integrate that information into students' own knowledge or schema. Given the temptation to simply restate or copy/paste material verbatim from texts or presentations, students need to learn how to use note-taking to critically synthesize and reformulate texts or presentations in their own words related to their own purposes or schema. Students therefore need to know how to use note-taking to reflect on their reading, viewing, or listening. This involves going beyond simply restating or regurgitating information to formulating their own beliefs and ideas. To help students distinguish between information and their own values, students can employ the split-page approach to note-taking. On the left side of the page, they record their initial perceptions or summaries of a text or presentation, and then, on the right side, they annotate, reflect on, or question those original impressions.

Students can use note-taking to develop material for writing drafts for essays. They can use digital note-taking tools such as Zoho Notebook, Evernote, Notetaker, Diigo, FreeMind, KeyNote, Webnotes, or Journaler to copy and paste those notes into their drafts. (Students can also use some of these tools on mobile devices such as iPhones or Touchs for taking fieldnotes.) Unlike writing by hand, these tools allow students to copy and paste notes into their drafts, organize notes using category or keyword systems, clip or annotate material from Web sites, or share their notes when working on collaborative writing projects.

Using Fieldnotes to Study Events or Spaces

One type of note-taking involves the use of fieldnotes for capturing specific observations about a particular event or space, such as a school sports match, restaurant interaction, or community celebration (Sunstein & Chiseri-Strater, 2007). Anthropologists use fieldnotes to describe their perceptions of cultural practices they observe in a particular setting. In taking fieldnotes, students are engaged in what we've referred to as slowing down to capture concrete observations or "verbal snapshots" of behaviors, objects, talk, settings, and so on at a event or site.

To introduce students to using fieldnotes, they could observe a local fast food restaurant, taking dual-entry fieldnotes. On the left side, they record specific aspects of the décor, people, conversations, ordering rituals, language, and so forth. On the right side, for each of the observations, either during or at a later time, they reflect on the social or cultural patterns they notice. For example, in recording that customers at a McDonald's restaurant employ shorthand language for placing their orders—"Big Mac and fries to go"—they then reflect on the fact that customers learn to use this shorthand from frequently patronizing McDonald's and that this form of ordering is very different from ordering in a more formal, upscale restaurant. Students may also coordinate their taking of fieldnotes with taking audio recordings, photos, or videos of the event that serve to capture or complement their written observations.

In Ellen Austin's beginning journalism class at a high school in Palo Alto, California, students learn to use fieldnotes through conducting ethnographic analyses of events that occur during the day in their school. During one class period, students took fieldnotes about, for example, the types of cars in the school parking lot, the school's television news broadcasts, a glass-blowing class, a chess match, the ethnic diversity of teachers, a world language class, an AP statistics class, the band room, the types of birds flying overhead, cross-country running, the types of book bags carried by students, a study hall, a football game, an automotive repair class, and graffiti tagging.

The students then used their notes to write short essay descriptions of each site that were then published for the class. One student, Claire Guo, describes her visit to a mathematics class that was studying frequency data, a visit that alleviated her apprehension about studying statistics:

> Brightly colored posters and cool 3D drawings of words cover the white walls and one blue wall. Mr. Hawkins, the class teacher, warmly welcomes her in. The class begins an activity and students seem to recite numbers off of a handful of coins to each other, the room buzzing with their talking. After sitting in the back of the room for a few minutes trying to figure out what is going on, the teacher walks over to me and explains the activity to me. The students, split into small groups, were collecting the average of the years that the coins were made in. They found these averages from groups of 2, 5, 10, 15, and 30 coins. One student picks the coins out of the bucket as his or her partner waits, ready to type the years into a calculator and churn out an average. "Tell me the numbers," they shout across the room. After getting the average for each amount of coins, they mark their data on the five graphs drawn on the whiteboards and chalkboards in the room. . . . To my utter amazement, the class enjoys themselves as they complete the activity in a breeze. . . . In only 40 minutes time, my perception of AP Stats completely changes.

Claire effectively describes details about the class to capture the particular culture of that class.

To reflect on their notes, students could identify tensions evident in their observations, asking themselves the questions, "What surprised me? What intrigued me? What disturbed me?" (Sunstein & Chiseri-Strater, 2007, p. 106), leading them to engage in critical inquiry about their school and community spaces.

Students can also use fieldnotes to engage in critical inquiry/ethnography projects in which they study the culture of their school or neighborhood. For example, Melissa's students at North Community High School, Minneapolis, took fieldnotes describing people, behaviors, and artifacts they observed in their school and neighborhood. They then reflected on those notes using the Critical Response Protocol prompts described in Chapter 2. On the left side of their papers, under the title of "Literal" and the caption "What do you see?," students described their observations. On the right side of their papers was the column titled "Inferential/meta-cognitive," with the caption "What do you think? Feel? Ask?" One 10th-grade student, Raymond, noted in the right-hand column, after recording his observations around the building:

Why were there people running around chasing one another?—and why did I write that down? Why did I pay attention to people's race? Why are there really big satellites outside of our school? Is there cable? Why are there fences around our school courtyard?

Raymond is using his notes to pose questions about his school that trigger tensions within himself related to what it means to thrive in a school and community that appear to be highly restrictive. He wonders about his peers' engagement in classroom studies; issues of race and identity; his curiosity about resources the school has access to; and the look and feel of learning when there are fences constructed around the school building. As an "urban ethnographer," he is beginning to interrogate the high level of "physical control" in urban schools that often leads to "intellectual control" in the classroom (Weis & Fine, 2000), controls associated with prisonlike institutional practices.

Students can also use fieldnotes to develop material for writing literary texts. In her teaching, Melissa posed the question to her students, "How do our exterior landscapes reflect and impact our intellectual, emotional and spiritual psyches?" Given this overriding question, senior student Markela Jones used an MP3 digital recorder to create fieldnotes about observing a man on a North Minneapolis street near the school, notes that gave rise to her further reflections and questions leading to creating the poem "Heru."

Heru

(by Markela Jones)

At these newly built High Rises on Plymouth Ave,
My attention is drawn to this man.
Cowray shells bounce from his chest,
As he watches, and tries to imitate the moving feet of a petite woman.
My focus is now turned to his old Reeboks,
Black and beat up,
And then his hairy, and skinny, yet muscular legs.
Irritated from the sun beaming down,
Almost burning my skin
I am drawn to his gray shorts,
That were once pants,
but had been cut to satisfy the season.
Small feet, and beautiful eyebrows
I noticed as I thought to myself, "they've been waxed."
Sweat drenched him, giving his skin a sepia glow.
I imagine smelling his perspiring body,
Trying to compare it to something familiar.
Holding my breath, I shrivel my nose,
It isn't at all pleasant, or what I wished it to be.
His natural appearance grasped my attention,
And was confirmed when he spoke.
"My name is Heru."
Instantly, I thought, "Hero,"
"God."
He communicated this feeling,
Being connected,
Spiritually grounded,
And mentally rooted.
I didn't want him to stop talking,
I'd fallen in love with his words.

Markela's poem builds on her fieldnotes describing concrete details of Heru—"his hairy, and skinny, yet muscular legs," "gray shorts," "Small feet, and beautiful eyebrows," and "his perspiring body," details that both attract her to him as a human being while at the same time repulse her: "I shrivel my nose,/It isn't at all pleasant, or what I wished it to be." It is these details, captured through her fieldnotes, that lead Markela to recognize his unique, human qualities so that she doesn't simply ignore him as just another homeless stranger on the street, because "I'd fallen in love with his words": "My name is Heru."

She is also using the language of descriptive fieldnotes to develop poetic language that double-voices (Bakhtin, 1981) language use itself based on the words "Heru" and "hero": "Instantly, I thought, 'Hero,'/'God.'" Rather than dismissing him as just another stranger, she equates him with being a "hero" or "God," leading her to recognize his humanity and the need to establish a relationship with him. In the process, she translates her descriptive fieldnote language into use of poetic language that captures her feelings in confronting her own biases.

As Markela's poem shows, students can use fieldnotes to slow down, defer judgment, and acknowledge what's happening in their relationships with people and events, leading them to critical inquiry and reflection about their worlds.

Using Interviews to Verify Fieldnotes

Students may also use interviews to verify or corroborate their fieldnotes with peers who observe the same people or events. After completing their notes, students could share observations/reflections with peers or the people they observed to ask if they agree or disagree with those observations/reflections. For example, if a group of students take fieldnotes of who's sitting with whom in the school lunchroom, leading to reflections about self-segregation according to race, class, or gender differences, students could share their insights with both their peers and with other students.

In conducting interviews, students need to employ open-ended questions so that interviewees express their honest feelings about themselves or an event. While they should prepare questions in advance, they also need to be open to adding new or follow-up questions. In a magazine journalism class with Ellen Austin, Ian Kelly learned how to employ note-taking, interview sheets, and story outlines in creating magazine stories, as well as the need to press sources for further background information. In a story, "The Forgotten Ones" (Kelly, 2008), published in the school's sports magazine, *The Viking*, Ian wrote about three basketball players, Brook Seaman, Brian Karvelas, and Connor Baskauskas, and their decisions not to play during their senior year, despite that when they were 10th graders their team won the California state high school basketball championship.

In the story, Ian draws on interview quotes to explore the reasons why the three players lost interest in the sport: Brook switched to playing football; Brian, to cross-country; and Connor, to playing on a National Junior Basketball team. Ian quotes Connor: "It was a huge time commitment and it became something that I was starting to not look forward to. . . . For me, playing at that high school level was no longer a recreational activity, it had become almost a chore" (p. 38).

Ian describes his experience in writing "The Forgotten Ones":

In the "Forgotten Ones", I interviewed Brian, Brook, Connor, a couple of additional players, one former coach, and Coach Diepenbrock. On the whole, interviews were critical to this story. Before writing, I felt I had a pretty good picture of what it would be like. However, the interviews unveiled a lot of information that I had not previously known of, and so they significantly altered the overall structure and tone of the story.

In addition, because of the story's complexity and the multiple sources involved, I would frequently follow up with sources to confirm or elaborate on certain information. Since Diepenbrock was essentially the figure of authority in this story, his interview was the most important. Any statement by one of the three would have to be echoed by Diepenbrock. This was especially significant because a lot of the story reflected on events that had taken place up to six years in the past, so with Diepenbrock corroborating what the players remembered, in turn the information I presented about middle school basketball became validated. The Diepenbrock and three player interviews were vital to the fall-out part of the story, especially because I was concerned that Diepenbrock's assessment would conflict with Brook, Brian and Connor's with regard to their departure(s) from basketball. However, for the most part their assessments were very similar, which was beneficial to the overall piece by avoiding any lingering controversy.

The interviews also were very undefined in terms of questions—I had known the basics behind the three players' basketball careers, but I didn't really know their various reasons for quitting or the details behind their paths toward success. Thus, these questions elucidated a lot of the gray spots in the initial story outline, and provided the emotional side to each of the players—each had separate motivations for playing, each had a strength that had brought them so far, and each had a differing view toward basketball. I think it was these three perspectives, facilitated by Diepenbrock's role as somewhat of a storyteller, which made the "Forgotten Ones" the story that it is.

Rather than simply rely on his own explanations of the students' reasons to forego playing their senior year, Ian's interviews provided him with insights into the players' and coach's perspectives for their decision to stop playing on the high school team. This use of interviewing to verify one's fieldnote observations is not only an essential literacy tool in journalism, but also as a means of conducting research.

MAPPING

Another reflective writing literacy tool involves mind-mapping—drawing circles or squares linked together to visually depict relationships between different topics and ideas. Students use mind-mapping to visually explore how topics and ideas are similar to, illustrate, contrast with, oppose, or build on one another. In addition to drawing maps, students can create maps using digital mapping tools such as Inspiration, Bubbl.us, Curio 2.4, VUE, and IHMC CmapTools. One advantage of using digital mapping is that students can view the material on their maps from a range of different perspectives. For example, with frequently used Inspiration, students can view maps from either a "diagram" or an "outline" perspective. With a diagram perspective, students create a "main idea" that appears in an initial circle and then create other related ideas around the main idea. They can also import symbols, pictures, images, and digital clips, including QuickTime movies and MP3 files, into their maps. Switching to the outline view transforms the material into a hierarchical outline with main topics and subtopics.

Students may use mind-mapping to define their allegiances to different social worlds they inhabit—their identities in the worlds of school, family, peer group, community, workplace, and so on, worlds represented by different circles or squares. As is the case with "you are here" geographic maps in shopping malls and towns, students may depict alliances with particular worlds in terms of how they adopt the beliefs and norms operating in each world. For example, for a year students in April Stasko's 11th-grade English class at a small-town Minnesota high school worked on the theme of identity construction. At the beginning of the class, students completed freewriting about their perceptions of their different roles related to worlds they participated in or inhabited. They first listed these roles, different activities, groups, or phenomena that contributed to their identity construction. They then combined these lists into categories according to places and people.

Students then created maps, using circles or squares to represent their different worlds. Based on questions provided by April, students reflected on their maps in terms of lack of connections between their worlds, identity definitions, the importance of certain places, the accuracy of their maps, and changes in their allegiances to different worlds. This led them to an understanding of how their identities are constituted through participation in different worlds.

In summary, we believe that reflective writing literacy tools help students learn to use writing to focus their attention in a sustained manner, create a record of their own thoughts, capture specific details based on observations, reformulate ideas from reading or lectures into their own words, visually depict ideas using mind-mapping, and share their ideas with others to receive feedback. While it is certainly important that students also learn to organize, revise, and edit their drafts as part of formal writing instruction, we believe that using the more informal literacy learning tool of reflective writing is equally important in helping students generate and reflect on ideas.

In using these tools, students need to bracket concerns about editing or readability because they are primarily using these tools for themselves. Thus, in giving feedback to this more informal writing, teachers and peers need to adopt an equally informal, conversational stance, posing questions that serve to foster further thinking about a topic or issue.

NINE

Images and Video

Envisioning the World

> Instead of just recording reality, photographs have become the
> norm for the way things appear to us, thereby changing the very
> idea of reality and of realism.
> —Susan Sontag, *On Photograpy*, p. 28

> When people talk to me about the digital divide, I think of it
> not so much about who has access to what technology as about
> who knows how to create and express themselves in the new
> language of the screen. If students aren't taught the language of
> sound and images, shouldn't they be considered as illiterate as
> if they left college without being able to read and write?
> —George Lucas, quoted in Daly, "Life on the Screen," p. 2

In her eighth-grade language arts class at Clara Barton School, located in a
diverse urban Minneapolis neighborhood, Amber Damm, 2009 Minnesota
Teacher of the Year, had her students focus on issues of civil rights portrayed
in *To Kill a Mockingbird* (Lee, 1960/2002), Langston Hughes's poetry, and
Dr. Martin Luther King's speeches in order to reflect on how writers use
visual metaphors to convey the need for civil rights, for example, Dr. King's
metaphors in "Letter from a Birmingham Jail"—the "disease of segregation," "depressing clouds of inferiority," "cup of endurance," and "abyss
of injustice." These visual metaphors function as powerful literacy tools
in helping readers equate concepts with a visual reference. After the students identified metaphors in their reading, they wrote their own metaphor
around concepts such as freedom, dignity, and racism, and represented these
through poems and drawings that were displayed in the school's hallways.
One student, Madelaine, illustrated her poem, "Inequality and Justice are
keen-eyed men/but inequality judges with his eyes/and Justice closes his
instead" with such a drawing (see Web site for images).

Her peer, Robin, wrote her poem: "Poverty is the spreading mist that envelopes mountaintops of pride, but strength is the lambent sunbeams piercing the mist and setting hope free," represented with a picture of the sun breaking through a misty field. Jack's poem, "Hope is the long bridge across the rushing river of injustice," was paired with a visual image of a bridge over a river. And Shira accompanied "Racism is lives hanging on a clothesline of inequality drying in the scorching sun/Clinging onto the remainder of their lives/Grasping for hope/Blowing in the violent winds of malevolence" with a drawing of a clothesline.

These eighth-grade students respond to powerful imagery with their own visual and written representations. As we noted in Chapter 7, images and videos involve the digital literacies of multimodality, interactivity, hyperlinking, and connectivity. For example, students are embedding, remixing, or linking to digital images from Flickr, Google Images, or Picassa and to videos from YouTube to create multimodal texts. In composing and designing their works, students can draw on an increasing number of images or video with Creative Commons copyright licenses, which allow for fair use by students in classrooms if they properly credit the producer. (For information about educational uses of Creative Commons, see the Creative Commons ccLearn license project [http://learn.creativecommons]).

Effective use of images and videos also involves an understanding of photographic techniques—the design, formatting, and color in images, as well as the use of angles, shot selection (close-ups, establishing, and medium shots), and editing in video (Beach, 2007; see http://teachingmedialiteracy.com for examples of analysis activities). All these conventions help create meaning.

Images and videos can have a powerful emotional effect on audiences that can serve to challenge and change perceptions. For example, the documentary series *Eyes on the Prize* (Hampton, 1987) influenced beliefs about the enduring significance of the civil rights movement, and films such as *Brokeback Mountain* (Lee, 2005) and *Milk* (Van Sant, 2008) can help shift attitudes about homosexuality. The establishing shot of *Brokeback Mountain* invokes the traditional American landscape, with the trope of the boundless frontier, but the film repopulates and reterritorizes this geography with more diverse gendered identities.

RESPONDING TO IMAGES

A useful first step in using images or video is for students to describe specific reactions to images or video using the Visual Thinking Strategies (VTS) approach, based on research by Abigail Housen (2007). As is the case with the Critical Response Protocol described in Chapter 2, students are asked to initially consider, "What's going on in this image?" or "What emotions do you associate with this image?" Based on these dimensions, students are asked to make inferences about the meaning of the images alongside questions such as, "What in the image made you think X?" or "What are you seeing that suggests X?" as well as "What's missing or left out of this picture?"

Students are also encouraged to describe features of design, color, texture, placement of objects, and positioning of the viewer with questions such as "What's near to you, far away, and in between?" or "What colors are used and how do you respond to those colors?" Furthermore, students speculate about the artist's or photographer's intent by considering, for example, "What did the artist or photographer do to make you see that?" or "What do you think the artist or photographer is saying about this event or society?" Students may also identify the artist or photographer and make connections to their entire body of work, including predominant stylistic features or thematic messages. These questions have resonance beyond the immediate academic exercise to other aspects of students' lives.

In working with her 12th-grade students in a visual arts animation course at the Perpich Center for Arts Education, Arts High School, Golden Valley, Minnesota, Colleen Brennan describes her use of the VTS with an animated video, *Calypso*, created by a student in the school. The video features two students playing a chicken and a pig and preparing to go to sea in a boat.

The students were given the opportunity to view the animation completely once before Colleen began asking the standard VTS questions that she framed for this medium: "What is going on in this animation?" "What do you see that makes you say that?" "What more can we find?" After the initial viewing, Colleen played the animation on a repeating loop, but muted the sound so students could discuss the piece at her prompting with the questions. As is common practice in all her classes, Colleen also gave students an opportunity to write their thoughts down before beginning the discussion.

During the whole-class conversation, Colleen encouraged students to refer to specific features of the animation to back up their theories about the symbolism and meaning of the piece. The animation played throughout the discussion, and students took control as they moved about the room to pause or rewind the piece in order to make a point or to highlight specific visuals as they articulated their theories. Students hypothesized what the chicken and pig characters symbolized according to popular vernacular and cultural references, as well as about the mythological ties of Calypso to the sea as the captor of Odysseus. Many students also discussed the symbolism of humans concealing their identities and of the masks "taking over" or possessing the humans.

This exercise prompted students to consider which metaphors and visual elements they could incorporate in their independent pieces. By structuring the conversation around the VTS questions, the viewing/meaning-making process was slowed. This allowed students to articulate connections between the visual representations they witnessed on-screen, the symbolism behind the actions/characters, and the meaning of the piece. The work of Colleen and her students highlights how Visual Thinking Strategies can be successfully incorporated into the classroom using moving works such as films and animations in the same way as they are used with still works like paintings, sculptures, photographs, and drawings.

Colleen uses VTS as a critical inquiry literacy tool to help students respond to the multimodal, symbolic meanings of the video images. The various modes in the animation exist in a synergistic relationship, and work together to provide opportunities for students to create meanings and interpretations.

Critically analyzing imagery extends to many disciplines. In studying famous photographers (http://www.masters-of-photography.com/summaries .html) in her class as part of the DigMe program at Roosevelt High School, Minneapolis, described in the Introduction, Delainia Haug asks students to respond to images using the following prompts:

1. What do you see? Start with the literal. List only tangible things— not ideas, feelings or conclusions. (For example, you can see a smile, but you cannot see happiness.)
2. Make three supported inferences from the photo. I think _____ because I see _____.
3. Do some analysis and make predictions. If you were in the photo, what would you be thinking, hoping and wondering? If you asked a person in the photo a question, what would they answer? Support your analysis with photographic evidence and background knowledge.
4. What does the photo tell you about the time and place, and these people?
5. What is missing from the photo? What do you think has been cropped out of the image? What questions do you have about what's outside the frame?

Students applied their analysis of photographic techniques in descriptive writing in their blog posts. For example, in response to an image of women sewing (for the picture: http://msamericadigme.blogspot.com/2008/12/photographer-blog.html), America noted that:

> I find this picture a very interesting and special one, because it shows the poor and hard times of New York City. You can see this by looking past the people and dirty walls. The children only got paid 2 to 3 cents each pair of pants they made. I believe the photographer was trying to say that kids as little as seven had to work hard and dirty jobs to make a living. She used this dark and dirty room to show the poor work places they had to work in. I think most little kids that lived in the city had to work, because they parents didn't make enough or was unable to work. That's why I believe this photographer took pictures of child labor.
>
> A good technique I think she used was the black and white. I like this technique because I believe it makes the picture more meaningful, it makes the picture that much more depressing. Another technique she used that caught my eye was the lighting; it's focused directly on them and not like the back room. She also used the proximity technique because she didn't focus the camera on another thing that wasn't important. I like how she had all of their heads down and frowning to show that they weren't having fun, so she did a wonderful job with the mood.

In her response, America describes how through this image the photographer documented poor working conditions through use of color, lighting, and proximity. America is beginning to discover that there are different historical and cultural models/understandings of what constitutes childhood. The photograph makes real and vivid that in many places and times, children are not merely consumers but also producers whose exploited work contributes to the family's survival.

In his analysis of Jerry Uelsmann's black-and-white photo of a 19th-century room with clouds at the top of the room (http://chrishoskyn.blogspot.com), Christopher noted that:

> There could be many different opinions on what this photograph is about. I think that it is saying that inside a perfect home there are things that people don't want others to see. In this photograph, I think that the major techniques used by Jerry Uelsmann include the lighting, mood and color. Or in this case lack there of. Had this picture been

taken in color, which it easily could have, I think it would lose some of the effect of the message. People would have been distracted by colors and may not have gotten the full message of this image. The lighting in the photo also makes the scene feel somewhat more depressing. If the artist had used different techniques such as taking the photograph from a different point of view the effect would have lost some of the feeling behind it. Also the framing is interesting. The entire message behind the photograph could have been completely different. Also if the sky effect had been left out this photo would be much harder to interpret.

Christopher is beginning to think like a photographer, noting the use of color and lighting to evoke particular feelings. The students are interpreting the symbolism of the artists' works, not unlike traditional literary analysis. These are not add-on skills, but an integral part of a complete humanities education.

CRITICAL INQUIRY OF IMAGES OR VIDEO

To encourage her students to engage in critical inquiry of media representations, Delainia asked them to consider the content of images and video through questions such as: "Who created this message?" "What creative techniques are used to attract my attention?" "How might different people understand this message different from me?" "What lifestyles, values, and points of view are represented in, or omitted from, this message?" "What is the message being sent?"

Posing these types of questions and noting consistent patterns in media portrayals provide opportunities for students to critique misrepresentations of everyday experiences. In her blog post, Samatha (http://bakkedigme .blogspot.com/2008/09/media-representations.html) described her class's analysis of media representations of the family related to gender and class differences:

We watched a couple of video clips of the (T.V.) American family in our class. I thought it was really interesting how they all had the same basic family lay out: one mother, father, 2 or more children, and often times a pet.

Another interesting thing I noticed was that the dad was always in charge and the mom was the type of person that couldn't do anything for herself. . . .

Another 2 clips I found very funny were the Folgers coffee commercials; one was from the 50's and one was from the 70's. Even though the two commercials took place 20 years apart they had the same basic story line: Wife couldn't make coffee, her whole life was wrapped around making a good cup of coffee to make her husband happy, and in the end all worries are gone when the wife made Folgers Instant coffee and the husband loved it. This gave me the sick feeling that they actually believed that because she made a good cup of coffee that her husband loves her more because he loves her coffee.

So I find it's interesting how different the media's view of family is compared to what us as a class came up with. For example, media views: 2 parents, rich/upper mid class, dad's in charge. Our views: 1 parent, poor/lower class, parent in charge.

I think that the media's perception of family is nice but unrealistic. It makes it seem like every family is well off. But as it is today even families that have 2 parents and both have jobs many of them are going through bad things such as losing their houses and cars.

Analysis of the visual medium enables students like Samatha to unpack gender, class, and capitalist ideologies in media portrayals, where the "health of a family" hinges upon proper consumption of branded products. This is a starting point for intersectional cultural analysis and critique: looking at the ways in which feminist issues, heteronormativity, and class instantiate themselves in commercialized interpretations of family. This then leads to questions about who produces these images, in what context, and for what purposes, leading students to advocate for more nuanced, accurate, and just representations of people and communities.

IDENTITY CONSTRUCTION

Students can consider how images/video are used to construct identities or how the body is portrayed or represented through talking, gesturing, standing, or moving in ways that evoke certain emotions—fear, anger, resentment, love, envy, desire, and so forth (Misson & Morgan, 2006). And they can consider how the identities portrayed reflect certain historical or economic forces.

One avenue for student inquiry is investigating how images of the self are shaped by gendered and racialized categories. Phil Halpern, an English teacher at a high school in the Bay Area, California, engaged with students in a curriculum experience called the "Phake Foto" project, intended to surface and unsettle conceptions of a stable, individual "self." As recounted by a graduate student researcher, Jessica Parker, to Richard, the purposes of the project included 1) getting to know other students in the class, 2) discussing issues regarding diversity and prejudice, 3) immersing students in some beginning and intermediate Adobe Photoshop techniques, and 4) discussing the purposes of and approaches to group projects. Phil first invited students to write about the ways people misunderstand their appearance and how appearance defines (or not) who you are. He then gave them the following task: each group takes a head (close-up) shot of all its members from the collarbones up and, using Adobe Photoshop, creates a hybridized face comprised of parts from all group members' photos. Three students— Valarie, Aaron, and Nader—combined their likenesses to create a composite photograph, which they named "Valaader" (see Web site for image).

In this project, students are realizing that racial categories are in many ways an arbitrary social convention that maps onto neither phenotype nor lineage. As Phil noted, from engaging in this project, students "eventually come to understand that notions of identity are fluid and one can play with or subvert agreed-upon interpretations and assumptions about identity or ethnicity and come to get a fresh look at what things mean."

Students can also inquire into how and why they use certain avatar images to project their identities on social networking or virtual game sites. For example, on the Whyville virtual science learning site, 8- to 16-year-olds create their avatars using face-part images to construct their identities (http://kafai-whyville.blogspot.com). Researcher Deborah Fields described in an interview with Richard how, after members had developed some ownership of the looks they had created, teachers challenged them to a costume contest. For one week they had to dress with a very different "look" on Whyville. In some cases, males adopted female identities; students also assumed identities as anime figures or aliens. Deborah noted that changing their avatars changed their peers' perceptions of them:

> The boy who adapted anime parts was sought after by girls and made a friend who shared his interests in his favorite anime series. Ben, one of the boys who dressed as a girl, felt awkward when a girl befriended him and started to talk about "girl things" like handbags. He quickly changed back to a boy and explained why he had dressed that way. Lucetta, who had dressed as an alien, was told she was ugly, to which she responded with a "thank you" because she was trying to be ugly.
>
> This experience, perhaps unique to virtual environments where one can completely change one's appearance, was an opportunity to discuss with the teens how looks affected people's reactions toward

them and how they felt about that. In virtual realities, there is a bit more leeway to inhabit and explore different personas. One of the dissonances, however, is that even in this freer medium, there is still policing and bullying. A virtual world isn't a completely alternative world; many of the biases of everyday life are carried over.

Similarly, students in Diane Whiting's eighth-grade health class in Rockland County, New York, created avatars on Teen Second Life (Boss, 2009). They first created avatars as similar to their actual appearances as possible, and then others that mimicked the media's idealized images of beauty. Students analyzed data about normal body size/shapes as applied to Barbie dolls and GI Joe action figures, leading them to recognize, as Whiting noted, "that Barbie wouldn't have room for intestines" and "Joe would have 36-inch biceps" (p. 15). When asked to chose avatars for representing their identities in Teen Second Life, most students preferred those similar to their own actual appearance.

The activities we have highlighted here are designed to trouble assumptions about too closely tying identity to appearance and to foster critical analysis of visual stereotypes and distorted media portrayals of ideal bodies, unearthing topics such as how representations of beauty can lead to eating disorders, an issue addressed by curriculum materials developed by About Face (http://www.about-face.org). Incorporating visual tools in the curriculum can help students investigate the real beauty of human variance.

Using Digital Videos to Explore Identity and Engage in Critical Inquiry

In addition to responding critically to images, students can also design and produce digital videos to explore aspects of their identities and engage in critical inquiry. Technology advancements have made it possible for students to readily produce work using digital video cameras and editing software like iMovie or Windows Movie Maker. For example, in the UCLA Migrant Student Leadership Institute summer program, high school students created digital videos focused on addressing social issues (Scott Nixon, 2009). One group of three students used their digital story to focus on the issue of domestic violence. They found images of battered women to include in their video and, through the use of digital editing, juxtaposed those images with sounds of women moaning or screaming to dramatize the brutal effects of domestic violence perpetrated by husbands or boyfriends. While this approach was quite explicit and graphic, it had a rhetorical power. Scott Nixon noted that creating these digital stories enhanced students' sense of agency to influence others:

> With the tools of traditional and new media, the students researched problems they saw in their lives and related the causes of these problems to critical social theories on issues of oppression, dehumanization, and social injustices. Their new understandings of these causes helped them develop agentive identities as social activists who can affect change through their future participation as leaders in their communities. The students shared their digital stories with their families, friends, and school counselors, so that they, too, could rethink these social problems and how they could be changed. (p. 75)

In creating digital videos, students often work better in teams who collaboratively plan and shoot footage. They could begin with working just with stills, and then move to creating ads, movie trailers, animations, genre narratives, or digital storytelling productions (Ohler, 2007). In the process, students study the use and purposes of camera shots/angles, sound effects, lighting, music, and editing techniques in their own work or in feature films.

Students begin with planning their videos based on the use of the visual to convey their story or idea. They then create a script and/or storyboard to plan out specific shots, recognizing that they need not be locked into these plans. The next step is shooting the video, recognizing that they can edit out irrelevant material or rearrange the order of events. In editing, they are able to add in music, titles/credits, and special effects to give their video a certain look, for example, adding eerie sounds and slow motion to a horror video.

One useful option is animation, because students have total control over design of the content. In his 10th-grade English classes in a St. Paul, Minnesota, high school, Jon Loo has his students create digital videos based on material objects to explore different aspects of identity construction. Jon's students also created narrative videos that explore issues of identity and agency portrayed through documentaries that dramatized students coping with challenges in their lives. One documentary portrayed a Hmong student recalling when her grandfather was killed in Laos while trying to escape to the United States, a reminder of the personal and historical traumas students carry with them to the classroom that are often left unarticulated in a standardized curriculum that homogenizes experience. In a detective/crime video created by Amanda and Nalee, a suspect (Amanda) is convicted and sentenced to die. As she is strapped to an electric chair, the video portrays a series of autobiographical flashbacks that imbue her with the dignity of a human who has a history. At the last moment, news arrives that proves her innocence, so she is spared. This video raises profound questions about the morality of capital punishment. The technique of the flashback enabled both young filmmakers to foreground human dignity under inhuman conditions.

Reflecting on Uses of Digital Image and Digital Video Production

In work with digital images and videos, it is useful for students to reflect on their purposes for using certain images, shots, or editing techniques and to assess the effectiveness of such features within the context of the overall goals for the project. For example, in choosing to employ a close-up shot of a person's shaking hand, a student could describe reasons for use of that close-up—to show that the person is nervous. In her digital production classes at Jefferson High School, Elizabeth Boeser's students create an "artist statement for public display with the video" based on the following instructions:

> Create the statement to reflect your definition of video and how it relates to your point of view on the subject of your work. Include anything else that you would like to communicate to the audience about yourself, your artwork, the subject, or the video form.

Students evaluate their video by answering the following questions:

- To what extent does the completed work fulfill your artistic intent?
- What are its strengths and weaknesses?
- How did feedback affect the development of the work?
- Give at least two examples of technical problems you encountered and explain how they were resolved in the creation of the piece.

To determine whether they have fulfilled their intentions with regard to audience, it is helpful for students to receive specific feedback to particular images or scenes in their videos. One fruitful avenue for such input involves putting their images on VoiceThread, where students can receive either written or audio comments from peers and teachers. To obtain feedback for videos, students can use an annotation tool, VideoAnt (http://ant.umn.edu), which allows for responding to specific scenes. As they view the video, peers and teachers can pause it and write their comments; the student then sees an arrow indicating that a comment has been made. Students can then determine from this feedback how the audience understood their work and gauge the effectiveness of particular techniques. Through this work, students contribute to a larger conversation about social issues.

In conclusion, given the ubiquity of images and video in contemporary culture, students need to know how to critically respond to and produce their own images and videos, leading to a recognition of how images and video both reflect and shape cultural perceptions. In doing so, students can use Visual Thinking Strategy questions to focus attention on specific meanings of an image or video, as well as rhetorical analysis of how images or videos are being used to appeal to certain audiences. Students can then use images and videos in digital storytelling productions to portray their analyses of contemporary social and cultural issues.

TEN

Assessing Uses of Literacy Tools

Reflecting on What Really Matters

> We must learn to measure what we value, rather than value
> what we measure.
>
> —Colin Connor, "Keynote Address," p. 4

On a wall of a Philadelphia elementary school, the artist Eliseo Silva drew on students' experiences to create a mural—*Coming to America, Making It Better*—that portrays an Asian American child reading a book, out of which rise images of Rosa Parks and Dr. Martin Luther King (Campano, 2006). The creative process incorporated a number of literacy tools described in this book, demonstrating how they should not only be thought of as separate but also how they may be used together for a collective project. For example, the students shared their migrant and refugee narratives; they brought in items from their homes that they felt represented their personal and cultural identities; and they engaged in a number of drama activities, such as frozen tableaux, in order to inform the vibrant and colorful aesthetic representation of their neighborhood and community.

In the mural project, the students engaged in critical inquiry, posing questions that included: Who is an American? What have we learned from one another? And what are our obligations to one another and to the world? When Eliseo asked the mostly immigrant, migrant, and refugee children whom they imagined as the quintessential American, many immediately responded with Rosa Parks. The mural celebrates how immigrants—how all Americans—have benefited from the legacies of the African American civil and human rights movements. It also represents the contributions of many other people through a pictorial assembling of cultural artifacts and images suggested by the students, including Peruvian finger puppets, samba dance costumes from Brazil, and African masks.

Part of the mural's relevance for educators is the pedagogical ideal it conveys, one of mutual edification and collaborative celebration. By drawing on knowledge derived from their own diverse rich experiences, working alongside supportive adults, the students portrayed a vision that contrasts with both the dominant paradigm of assimilation and the view that society's different worlds are too segmented and isolated to understand one another. The mural is thematically balanced, representing cultural distinctiveness as well as overlapping history and shared interest. This includes the interest of all people in living free from oppression—oppression both outside and within our national borders—as symbolized in the mural by broken chains at the base of the Statue of Liberty.

Eliseo often describes how murals are a form of visual literacy that "activates space" (personal communication, April 20, 2009). They are a way for community members to aesthetically and conceptually reclaim public spaces from impersonal forces such as economic abandonment or gentrification. Through creating the *Coming to America: Making It Better* mural, the students literally became public intellectuals, creating a more nuanced representation of American culture and immigrant experience from which others might learn.

This is sophisticated and artful collective work. Unfortunately, the current assessment climate, which emphasizes individual aptitude through the testing and measurement of discrete decontextualized skills, provides little, if any, guidance for educators to respond to and build off the depth and complexity of student literacy tool use. A school fortunate enough to even have a mural project would most likely relegate it to "extracurricular" activities, outside the disciplinary domain of literacy learning, and therefore more apt to be cut during times of financial stress, along with the arts more generally. What is required is a more expansive understanding of both literacy and literacy tool assessment as a form of collaborative inquiry.

TOWARD CHANGE-BASED ASSESSMENT

In this final chapter, we discuss ways of assessing students' growth in their uses of literacy tools. We argue that the purpose of assessment should be to foster students' individual and collaborative self-reflections about their uses of literacy tools to engage in change of status quo spaces as well as their perspectives and sense of agency—what we describe as *change-based assessment*. We define change-based assessment as evaluating students not only on the intrinsic aspects of their work—whether, for example, their essays include "elaborated reasons" or their stories include creative use of dialogue—but also on the degree to which their literacy tool use results in change related to fulfilling any of the four purposes described in this book—change in the status quo resulting from critical inquiry, constructions of space, identity enactment, and/or sense of agency. By providing feedback, teachers can foster student reflection on the extent to which they have achieved any of these four purposes and reasons for (or for not) doing so. In this self-reflection, students repeatedly pose questions about both how and why their uses of particular tools allow them to achieve certain purposes and how they can improve on using those tools in the future. For example, considering their use of the mural as a visual literacy tool for engaging in critical inquiry, students could reflect on the degree to which their images conveyed the richness of previous generations' historical struggles in ways that change audiences' perceptions of their neighborhood. They may also ask themselves if the mural (re)presents the neighborhood in a way that challenges stereotypes and captures its complexity. In order to gauge the impact of the project, they may interview community members about how they view and understand the mural. Based on this information, the may develop new ways to engage in collective self-definition and advocate for neighborhood needs, such as a youth arts program.

Our notion of change-based assessment derives from, and extends, "3rd-generation assessment" theorists who argue that how one assesses depends on the kind of learning valued in society (Carr, 2001; James et al., 2006; Lewis, 2008; Swaffield, 2008). These theorists noted that the first generation of assessment focused primarily on whether students acquired predetermined transmitted knowledge by testing, a behaviorist model of learning that was valued in a world where people were trained to perform specific, disconnected, and mechanistic tasks. The second generation of assessment focused on students' cognitive processing of information and construction of understanding, for example, to establish if students can make correct inferences about a text or defend a thesis in a composition, a view of learning that values individual aptitude.

However, as we have argued in this book, succeeding in contemporary, networked, and participatory society involves going beyond such individual processing and acquisition of information to learn how to socially construct and represent cultural knowledge (Jenkins, 2006; Shirky, 2009; Siemens, 2008). As illustrated in the mural project, young people need to learn to work collaboratively with others. Third-generation assessment theorists focus on fostering authentic self- and group reflection on uses of literacy tools mediating participation in collaborative work driven by a shared belief in the need to make social changes. In describing assessment of writing literacy tools, Ernest Morrell (2008) argues that:

Students do not only need the tools to write correctly: they need a purpose for writing that extends beyond scholastic or professional success on the one hand, and a better understanding of themselves on the other. What students need is an association of composition with advocacy, with activism, with empowerment, and with revolution. (p. 134)

We also argue that rather than being after the fact, assessment needs to be an ongoing process that occurs during or alongside activities in ways that focus on both individuals and related group social practices (Swaffield, 2008). As students engage in any activity, they should have access to continuous, descriptive, supportive feedback from both teachers and peers, feedback that leads to self-reflection about how one is effectively using literacy tools and how one could improve in their use.

USE OF QUESTION-ASKING TO FOSTER SELF-REFLECTION

Central to self-reflection is the ability to pose questions about uses of literacy tools, questions such as the following: "How effective am I using this tool to engage my audience?" "How is my language capturing the attention of my intended audience?" "What might I or we do differently?" For example, one of the students in the online role-play described in Chapter 7 reflected on the effectiveness of their arguments in the virtual space of a debate about the school's Internet policies.

> Putting myself in the shoes of someone who has authority in the district helped me put myself through what they go through to make policy recommendations. By doing this I realized that these rules have to apply to a broad range of people, not just me. That is where my opinions changed and I realized that this issue is affecting more people than just me. Without the role play I would not have formulated the opinions that I did and it opened me up to the things that I didn't understand.

In reflecting on their capacity to engage in critical inquiry, students can assess their ability to establish the significance of a problem or issue by posing the following questions:

- Have I/we established the significance of this problem or issue to my audience based on arguments and supporting evidence?
- Will my/our audience perceive me/us as serious about addressing this problem or issue?

And in formulating possible solutions to the problems they are addressing, students could assess their effectiveness by posing these questions:

- Do our possible solutions adequately address the root causes of problems?
- Will our audiences perceive these proposed solutions as viable?

Students may also reflect on their effectiveness in working collaboratively with others. They may note the degree to which members of the group had a clear sense of their roles and responsibilities, as well as their willingness to each pull their own weight in completing their particular assignments. They may also reflect on their ability to network or make connections with people to assist them in their work by asking:

- Did members of our group have a clear sense of their roles and responsibilities and our shared purposes?
- How did working with others make a difference in achieving our shared purposes and my individual goals?
- How well did I collaborate with others?
- What were the challenges or difficulties our group faced?
- What did I do to address and overcome these challenges?
- How did we collaborate to effectively address and resolve difficulties?

Students can assess their effectiveness in using literacy tools to attempt or actually make change by reflecting on audiences' responses to their work. They may note the extent to which their writing, acting, artwork, performances, and so forth challenged or possibly even contributed to transforming their audiences' beliefs or perceptions of themselves or others. In an interview with Melissa, one of her former 12th-grade students, Michelle, described what she learned through writing and performing a poem about love and death as portrayed in the Greek play *Alcestis*. She reflects on how writing and performing the poem led to changes in her identity:

> I leave myself open to opportunities that will stretch me, and I grow and I become bigger and broader and maybe that's the way I cannot be classified by society, because I am so big and so out of the box that the complexity of myself cannot be put into a box.

Michelle recognizes how her performance led her to resist ascriptions that categorize her in limiting and dehumanizing ways.

Students may also consider their ability to make changes in their own school or community. Two 12th-grade students in Bloomington, Minnesota, Anna Tu and Farnaaz Farzanehkia, both daughters of immigrant parents, were concerned about their difficulties in learning to adjust, as outsiders, to a relatively closed, White, middle-class high school culture. On their own initiative, they wrote a letter identifying the problem they face in coping with the lack of mentoring and support for their schooling:

> Our parents did not have the experience or resources needed to guide us through our education. Although cultural barriers have greatly affected our lives, they are only one of the factors creating the achievement gap. The achievement gap can be described as a gap between the educational achievement measured by the performance of students with different gender, race/ethnicity, ability, and socioeconomic statuses. Many students grow up like us with cultural differences that become a barrier in their academic performance, others don't have money or resources available, and some don't even have the motivation to do well for various reasons.

Given this problem, Anna and Farnaaz proposed setting up a mentorship program with college students from the University of Minnesota who would interact in person or online with mentees regarding issues such as college applications and academic challenges. They noted a number of benefits from such a mentorship program:

> High school students will benefit from having a role model that inspires and motivates them to develop future goals. We would like to help students who may not have the desire to do well in school create the opportunity to realize the significant impact education will have on their future. In addition, the mentors can use their own experiences to advise students while earning volunteer hours. High school students often undergo stress, issues with friends or family, and a changing environment. Not only will the mentors deal with educational aspects of school, but they will also be a friend that a student can come to. Every participant will walk away knowing they have helped close the achievement gap.
>
> Our next step is getting the program approved by both Jefferson High School and the University of Minnesota. Once this is done, we will create an application and a contract which will contain expectations, rules, obligations, and an order for operation that should be followed when the program is introduced next year. Lastly, we will

network with teachers, administrators, and students from both schools to get the word out for the purpose of gaining participants. We are asking for your support regarding this opportunity so advice, ideas, or recommendations would be greatly appreciated.

Their teacher, Elizabeth Boeser, submitted their letter to Richard, a faculty member at the University of Minnesota, who was impressed by the quality of the letter and advocated on the students' behalf to university administrators, who subsequently have indicated an interest in setting up a mentorship program. Anna and Farnaaz went beyond voicing their frustrations and identifying a problem to proposing solutions and recruiting support.

As they worked on their letter, they continually reflected on how to craft a proposal that would be effective in achieving their goals. In her self-assessment of the effectiveness of their letter, Anna described her enhanced sense of agency associated with addressing a problem in her school leading to change:

> Throughout my life I have experienced many difficulties between my family and the cultural barriers that were instilled in being born as a second-generation Vietnamese immigrant. Since my parents and I were raised in two completely different worlds, the culture clash had set off certain disadvantages for me. Growing up I had always confided in my friend Farnaaz, who could relate to most of the struggles I had gone through. As the daughter of Persian immigrants, she had also gone through many of the obstacles that accompanied growing up with cultural differences. These were issues we could not talk to our other friends about because as American children, they would never understand. We would often let our struggles become unnoticed to the public and confide in each other whenever we needed support. Now that we are seniors in high school, we realized that the greatest lessons we learned in life came from enduring times of difficulty, overcoming struggle, and striving for the better.
>
> As we are about to embark on a new journey as college becomes near, we want to do something to leave our mark behind. We want to use our experiences to create change and improvements. We know that the problems we have encountered over the years are prevalent however unseen. The purpose of our proposal is to raise awareness to this issue and to take a step into helping others who may also be struggling. We focused our attention on the achievement gap because

it is something that we feel very deeply about. Our proposal includes our vision and plan for this program. We want to launch our ideas by showing that our plan could be highly effective. There is not enough being done about this matter, and we hope to inform others about this rising concern. After sending our proposal out to our administration, school advisors, and district supervisors, we are pleased to know that everyone is fully in support of what we are doing. It is our goal to bring attention to an issue that has gone unnoticed at our school and use our resources to create a program that will help close the achievement gap.

In her reflection, Anna describes how she and Farnaaz were initially reluctant to publicly express their concerns as daughters of immigrants. As seniors, however, they were willing to voice the need to address the achievement gap facing immigrant students in their letter because they felt that the knowledge gained from their own experiences could help future generations. They recognize that they have the agency to promote change by proposing a plan that would be perceived by their audiences as a viable first step. By defining their purposes for writing the letter in terms of the changes they want to achieve, Anna and Farnaaz create their own measure for future assessment.

Students may also reflect on their long-term development and evolving identities in an autobiographical mode, noting how their uses of literacy tools represented key turning points in their lives leading to an enhanced sense of agency. Donnie Belcher, described in Chapter 3, assessed her poetry-writing in high school as highly significant in providing her with the strength to go on to college at DePaul University. During her sophomore year, she went to Washington, D.C., read a piece at a *Dismantling the Cradle to Prison Pipeline* conference, and met one of her heroes, Maya Angelou. Donnie appeared in a *Children's Defense Fund—Beat the Odds* video and performed in a stage production of *For Colored Girls Who Have Considered Suicide/When the Rainbow Is Enuf* (Shange, 1977). She has since become a teacher in the Chicago Public Schools:

> I broke a cycle. . . . I learned, no matter what, you can bounce back, be resilient. Out of all this, I found what was most important. This is what I share with my students.

As an English teacher, Donnie sponsored a spoken-word club and focused much of her curriculum around autobiographical aspects of poetry and identity. Though she is not currently writing poetry ("My poet voice, she's quiet and on the inside of me now. She's in there, in my heart. I write now more for other people, than about me"), she now uses images and texts to create scrapbooks: "I think in poems, but I don't write them down anymore. My artistic energy has gone into visual art now, quilting. I make pages now, scrapbooks. . . . Then, it was creating who I was going to be—I was writing my way into a new identity. Now, it's capturing who I am."

Donnie's growth as an educator, artist, and activist adept at literacy tools could never have been plotted a priori by traditional school assessments, which too often are used to sort students on a bell curve, thereby delimiting their potentials and educational experiences through reductive generic categories ("the struggling learner" or the "gifted and talented student"). Donnie's profound journey is singular, and ultimately best assessed through processes of self-reflection.

To reflect on their ability to use literacy tools to achieve change, students could pose the following questions:

- What are those changes that I am trying to achieve—what are the purposes driving my uses of literacy tools?
- How am I using literacy tools to achieve these changes?
- To what degree am I successful in achieving change? If not, how might I modify my uses of literacy tools to more successfully achieve change?
- How did attempting to or actually achieving change enhance my sense of agency?

USE OF TEACHER AND PEER FEEDBACK TO FOSTER SELF-REFLECTION

Both teachers and peers play an important role in fostering student self-reflection. Teachers can chart students' abilities and proficiencies to be able to record shifts in their perspectives or sense of agency over time. For example, in writing about a 10th grade student in his North Minneapolis high school, Jamie Plaisance noted that:

> Roxanne is one of our most improved students. She has gone from in danger of failing all of her classes to boasting four A's, one B, and one C this quarter. She started the year hating to write, except for notes to friends and in her diary. But after journaling 2–3 times per week, she clearly takes joy in writing now. Last month, for instance, she entered a writing contest on her own volition that the Minnesota

Timberwolves were running. She won 4 game tickets for her compelling essay on Barack Obama. You can truly hear her voice and feel her emotion in her writing. Sometimes, my feedback for Roxanne is something like "how about periods?," but more often than not I just try to keep reminding her that she has talent. Lately, she is trying to live up to that belief.

By noting changes in Roxanne's interest in writing and in her voice, Jamie provided her with specific feedback about the effectiveness of her uses of writing as a literacy tool to express her ideas, an assessment that was validated in her competition win as she gained new confidence in herself as a writer.

A significant challenge teachers face, particularly with large class sizes, is how to provide individual feedback to every student. One alternative for teachers is to model, encourage, and show peers how to also provide specific, descriptive feedback that fosters self-reflection. However, without some training and careful scaffolding, peers may provide only general, laudatory, or overly judgmental feedback, which can be counterproductive. In her eighth-grade language arts class at a suburban Minnesota middle school, Dana Driessen had her students reflect on their narrative writing through peer conferencing. In framing her assignment, Dana stressed the importance of showing versus telling readers about their characters through the use of descriptions of protagonists' thoughts, actions, and dialogue.

She also structured peer conferences by devising questions and procedures to ensure that students provide positive and supportive specific feedback. After the students wrote their drafts, they paired up and asked each other questions that included the following: "What is your story about? Who is your main character? What conflicts do your main characters experience in the story? What point of view did you use? Why did you choose this particular setting?"

Partners read aloud the draft to the writer. While reading the story, the partner took notes on sections that "are *fabulous* [marked] with an '!' in the margin and not what is effective," and that "are confusing [marked] with a '?' and make a note of why it's confusing." In the context of this positive feedback, partners also noted the following: misspellings; paragraphs that were too long or short; and the need to combine, rearrange, delete, or clarify writing. Finally, partners reviewed these notes with the writer and provided the writer with responses to these questions: "What are two strengths of this story? What are two things that need work in this story? In this story, I want to know more about . . . In this story, I wondered why . . ."

Structured sharings like these also model how students may reflect on their own work. After they revised initial drafts, the students analyzed their own stories in terms of whether or not they achieved their intentions. For example, Jessica, who wrote about how she was able to create an authentic character:

> I am proud of this piece because I was able to really describe the character by telling a story. I also like that I was able to make the character seem like a real person, not just a character trapped in a cage. This piece was engaging because I was able to imagine a person's story in my head and then actually make it into a story. It was also engaging because of the level of descriptive writing that needed to be put into it.

In a reflection of her own alternative ending to the book *Twilight* by Stephenie Meyer (2006), another student described how she wanted to re-tain Meyer's style while creating her own ending:

> This was *a lot* of fun for me because I got to read a book I liked and do a project for instead of a book chosen for me. One of the challenges of this piece that I really enjoyed was trying to get into the author's style but still tell the story I wanted to tell. It was also kind of easy to make an alternative ending for the book because the characters were already well-established.

These students' self-reflections serve to enhance their sense of agency and awareness of their changing identities as effective writers who can gain satisfaction from their work.

USING LEARNING STORIES TO REFLECT ON LITERACY TOOL USES

In addition to posing questions or using teacher/peer feedback to foster self-reflection, teachers and students may also use narrative descriptions or "learning stories" (Carr, 2001, 2008) of their uses of literacy tools. Elizabeth Boeser (as we noted in Chapter 7) has her creative-writing students write "artist statements" as a form of "learning stories." They reflect on their story-writing just as they do about their video productions. Students de-scribe their story-composing processes and what they learned about writing stories. For example, a ninth-grade student, Abby Trevor, reflects on her experience of writing a fantasy short story:

I almost always write medieval fantasy stories. This story seemed like a good chance to vary from that a little bit, so I wrote a modern fantasy instead. It might not seem like that much of a change, but the style is different nonetheless, especially as this story was set on our Earth while most of my other stories are not. My goal was to gain more experience with a different kind of writing and improve my style in general.

It soon became clear, however, that I couldn't fit [my original ideas] in with the limits on the story's length. . . . I actually think that that was somewhat lucky. Hopefully this way, the reader can use their imagination to come up with some of the [characters'] previous adventures, but there's enough in the story so that they're not totally bewildered. My options are also open if I ever want to write a prequel or a sequel. Overall, I ended up getting rid of my broader ideas and focusing more on a few key scenes.

This naturally changed my perspective as well. I realized that I had to focus my attention and writing on the scenes that were absolutely necessary to the story.

Abby realizes that unlike her prior fantasy stories, her current story is set on Earth, thus requiring her to reference realistic settings, as well as employ a different style. She recognizes that, given potential audience responses, she needed to reduce the length of her story by highlighting significant events and reducing background information about characters, assuming that her audiences could infer information about her characters' backgrounds, lessons that will help her in her future story writing.

USING E-PORTFOLIOS TO FOSTER SELF-REFLECTION

Using e-portfolios is a particularly effective way for students to reflect on and assess their long-term growth in their uses of literacy tools (Barrett, 2009; Dimarco, 2006). E-portfolios consist of representative samples of students' work—writing, digital productions, images, videos, artwork, and so on—particularly over the period of a course or school year, along with students' reflections on how that work represents growth and development in their uses of literacy tools (for more information, see Helen Barrett's site: http://helenbarrett.com).

In the past, students created print-based portfolios containing paper files. Students can now use their blogs or a wiki as a digital repository of their work over the period of a course, academic year, or several years. While there are commercial e-portfolio platforms available, these platforms are often expensive and overly structured. If students are keeping their own blog or can create their own wiki, they then have more of a sense of ownership over their e-portfolio than with a commercial platform.

What transforms a blog or wiki into an e-portfolio is the additional self-reflection about their work, one that will vary depending on the purposes for keeping their e-portfolio. In some cases, an e-portfolio may be used to simply store all of their work, including drafts and related artifacts. In contrast, a "display" or "showcase" e-portfolio may contain only those items that they want to share with particular audiences. Students may also include certain material and reflect on their e-portfolio according to differences in their audience. For their teachers, they may include material and reflect on what they have learned, while for college admissions offices or future employers, they may include work that demonstrates their ability to succeed in college or in a workplace.

In assembling their e-portfolios, students can use a table of contents that helps audiences readily locate different samples of their work. They may also use hyperlinks to connect samples, connections that themselves foster reflections about similar themes they were addressing throughout a course. Students work together in small groups on their portfolios, sharing their reflections with one another. They might also have e-portfolio conferences with their teacher, who can ask students to verbally comment on their work. In "alongside" reflections, Jenny Lewis (2008) has students pose the following:

> Where could I (or we) look for help? What would I do differently? What would I like to do now? Why was I learning this? How did I react? What would I like to do now? What was good/not so good? Was there a problem? How could I fix my problem? What have I learnt about myself? Is it my fault something didn't work? Have I understood? What needs improvement? What do I need help with? What would I like to learn next? How can we help each other? What connections can I make with any other learning? Could I have done anything differently? Could I teach this to someone else? Was this interesting or boring—why? (pp. 4–5)

Teachers can provide students with questions such as those used by Jonathan Mueller (2008):

> Selection questions/prompts: Why did you select this piece? Why should this sample be included in your portfolio? How does this sample meet the criteria for selection for your portfolio? I chose this piece because . . .
>
> Growth questions/prompts: What are the strengths of this work? Weaknesses? What would you work on more if you had additional time? How has your _____ (e.g., writing) changed since last year? What do you know about _____ (e.g., the scientific method) that you did not know at

the beginning of the year (or semester, etc.)? Looking at (or thinking about) an earlier piece of similar work, how does this new piece of work compare? How is it better or worse? Where can you see progress or improvement? (pp. 16–17)

This questioning process may help students to select those examples of their work that best illustrate their strengths, weaknesses, learning, and growth. It is also useful to have students propose future developments in their work.

- How is using the wiki (or another particular literacy tool) making a difference in your/our involvement in our project?
- From what people have written on the blog (or other literacy tool that encourages dialogue), how do you think the reactions of our audience—the people we are trying to reach—are (or were) changing?

TEACHER SELF-ASSESSMENT

One important caveat in assessing students' efforts in making change within a community is that teachers themselves benefit from reflecting on how their own beliefs influence their evaluation of students. And it is through self-reflection and systematic inquiry and research into their teaching that teachers grow as professionals (Cochran-Smith & Lytle, 2009). For example, Janie Sammons, one of the first-grade teachers working with Brian, reflects on how she was positioning a student, Colin, in ways that were counterproductive, a realization that led her to change her perceptions of him and his identity/agency in her class:

All year I had tried to make Colin into something he was not. When he presented all those ideas he had collected I suddenly realized that he saw himself as an historian for our class. Then I could better help him extend his writing, and support his participation, especially in interviewing others, as well as in recording and presenting his ideas. It comes back to asking ourselves who are we doing this for? Where are we going? What are the possible avenues to get there? I really have to remember to listen and respond to what the kids want, need, are already capable of doing, and their ideas about where we can go. When my responses are "Yes, and . . ." I can really support students to achieve what they envision in the ways they choose, so that they can grow into becoming the people that we may never have imagined they could be.

Janie's reflection does not focus on deficit-driven assessments, but attends to her individual students' unique alchemies of talent as a launching pad for their growth. This shift entails that educators constantly question their own preconceptions of students, limited by assumptions about what students know and "need to know," as opposed to being open to another human being's abilities or potential to supersede expectations.

This shift also involves opportunities for young people and teachers to become more interconnected and caring human beings, listening and attending to the spoken, written, performed, and digitally recorded voices of others both within school walls and, via the Internet, from around the world and across time. The teachers whose work we highlight use literacy tools to create, on a daily basis, ethical, creative, and intellectual public spaces for collaborative inquiry and social change.

As educators, we should strive for a plurality of voices in our classrooms, particularly ones typically excluded from the school curriculum, and refrain from putting students' experiences in boxes with labels such as "struggling reader," "the geek," "the loser," "the foreigner," "the illegal," or "the doomed-to-fail" derived from limited test data or cultural presuppositions. Rather, we should provide opportunities for personal and collective self-definition. Maribel, whose narrative we shared in Chapter 1, is emblematic of how much we have to learn from everyone in our increasingly interconnected world.

In a conversation with Gerald during final revisions to this book, Maribel reflected on her own narrative. "If you want to further understand my story, you might also read this," she suggested. Maribel handed Gerald a copy of *Los Sueños de America*, a short story anthology about migration by the award-winning Peruvian writer Eduardo González Viaña (2000). The gesture was a reminder that individuals bring their own rich conceptual frameworks to interpret their experiences and practices, and that educators—researchers and teachers alike—ought to learn from, not merely analyze and assess from above, those with whom they work. Maribel also offered the following opportunity:

And if you *really* want to understand, you should spend time with my extended family in the United States, hear all their stories, how they got here, their aspirations and challenges. Return to your roots. Return to Queens (the New York borough where much of her family resides, and where Gerald's own grandparents had migrated from the Philippines and Italy).

Maribel suggests that true knowledge is the result of accretive collective wisdom, not merely individual expertise. Perhaps most importantly, Maribel reiterated the reason she shared her narrative in the first place: "I want others to hear these stories so that we can provide more support and resources for immigrants and their families."

For Maribel, storytelling is a tool for activism, a way to bring about positive change in the world and in herself. Similar to Donnie, Anna, Farnaaz, and all of the other talented young people featured in this book, Maribel is motivated by an ethical vision larger than her own individual advancement. She teaches us that we are all interconnected and that education is fundamentally about the well-being of everyone and the flourishing of future generations. That is what really matters and what ultimately should be assessed. We believe educators should follow these young people's leads to bring about positive change. Our hope is that the literacy tools featured in this book will be useful to others' collaborative projects of transformation.

INVITATIONS AND RECOMMENDATIONS

We close this book with an invitation to contribute your own examples of activities, lesson plans, and student work, as well as links or further reading, to our wiki resource site: http://literacytooluses.pbworks.com. (To add material to this wiki, readers need to set up an account with pbworks.com; they can also e-mail Richard at rbeach@umn.edu to request access to edit).

We also recommend that teachers in all subject-matter areas share their experiences in employing literacy tools with one another so that literacy learning permeates all areas of the school curriculum. By using the literacy tools described in this book in all of their classes, students, as did Anna and Farnaaz, acquire a sense of competency in their ability to employ literacy tools to achieve change.

And we note the need to continually recognize that the uses of digital literacy tools we describe in this book may, 10 or 20 years from now, be used in new and different ways as we move further into a digital age. At the same time, other literacy tools—narratives, drama, spoken word, writing, images, and so on—will also continue to evolve as people create new uses for these tools to achieve new purposes (Leander, 2009). All of this suggests the need to encourage students to continually improvise in their uses of literacy so that they themselves foster novel uses of tools, given the need to address future issues and challenges.

CONCLUSION: THE IMPORTANCE
OF PURPOSE IN USING LITERACY TOOLS

We conclude by reiterating our primary focus on the importance of using literacy tools to achieve valued purposes related to engaging in critical inquiry, constructing spaces, enacting identities, and achieving a sense of agency. Focusing on these rationales for using literacy tools shifts the focus of literacy instruction from instrumental acquisition of how to use these tools—how to write a story, adopt a role, perform a poem, create a blog post, take field notes, or make a video—to also knowing how these tools can be used to fulfill larger purposes. By continually defining and reflecting on their purposes for using literacy tools, students recognize, as did Douglass and Maribel, that these tools are leveraged to make changes in themselves and the world.

As students gain confidence in their ability to use the literacy tools described in this book, they perceive themselves as problem-solving change agents who value literacy for defining their identities and improving their lives.

References

Achebe, C. (1988). *Hopes and impediments: Selected essays*. New York: Anchor Books.

Alcoff, L. M. (2005). *Visible identities: Race, gender, and the self*. New York: Oxford University Press.

Alim, H. S. (2006). *Roc the mic right: The language of hip hop culture*. New York: Routledge.

Allison, P. (2009). Be a blogger: Social networking in the classroom. In A. Herrington, K. Hodgson, & C. Moran (Eds.), *The new writing: Technology, change, and assessment* (pp. 93–110). New York: Teachers College Press.

Anson, C., & Beach, R. (1995). *Journals in the classroom: Writing to learn*. Norwood, MA: Christopher Gordon.

Baker, H. (1980). *Journey back*. Chicago: University of Chicago Press.

Bakhtin, M. M. (1981). *The dialogic imagination* (M. Holquist, Ed., C. Emerson & M. Holquist, Trans.). Austin, TX: Texas University Press.

Barajas, H. L., & Ronnkvist, A. (2007). Racialized space: Framing Latino and Latina experience in public schools. *Teachers College Record, 109*(6), 1517–1538.

Barrett, H. (2009). Electronicportfolios.org. Retrieved July 6, 2009, from http://helenbarrett.com

Beach, R. (2007). *Teachingmedialiteracy.com: A guide to resources and activities*. New York: Teachers College Press.

Beach, R., Anson, C., Kastman-Breuch, L., & Swiss, T. (2009). *Teaching writing using blogs, wikis, and other digital tools*. Norwood, MA: Christopher Gordon.

Beach, R., & Doerr-Stevens, C. (2009). Learning argument practices through online role-play: Toward a rhetoric of significance and transformation. *Journal of Adolescent & Adult Literacy, 52*(6), 460–468.

Beach, R., Haertling-Thein, A., & Parks, D. (2008). *High school students' competing social worlds: Negotiating identities and allegiances in response to multicultural literature*. New York: Routledge.

Beach, R., & Myers, J. (2001*). Inquiry-based English instruction: Engaging students in life and literature*. New York: Teachers College Press.

Bernstein, M., & Greco, D. (2009). *Reading hypertext*. Cambridge, MA: Eastgate Systems.

Biesta, G., & Tedder, M. (2007). Agency and learning in the lifecourse: Towards an ecological perspective. *Studies in the Education of Adults, 39*(2), 132–149.

Bolton, G. (1999). *Acting in classroom drama: A critical analysis.* Portsmouth, NH: Heinemann.

Bonilla-Silva, E. (2001). *White supremacy and racism in the post-civic rights era.* Boulder, CO: Lynne-Rienner.

Boss, S. (2009). Avatars teach teens about self-image. *Edutopia, 5*(3). Retrieved June 30, 2009, from http://www.edutopia.org/digital-generation-self-image-avatars

Botel, M. (2008). An open letter to all those who may influence the new educational policies of federal, state and local governments. Retrieved on February 22, 2009, from http://www.gse.upenn.edu/pln/

boyd, d. (2006). A blogger's blog: Exploring the definition of a medium. *Reconstruction: Studies in Contemporary Culture, 6*(4). Retrieved March 16, 2007, from http://reconstruction.eserver.org/064/boyd.shtml

Brannon, L., Griffin, S., Haag, K., Iannone, T., Urbanski, C., & Woodward, S. (2008). *Thinking out loud on paper: The student daybook as a tool to foster learning.* Portsmouth, NH: Heinemann.

Bruner, J. (1996). *The culture of education.* Cambridge, MA: Harvard University Press.

Bulosan, C. (1974). *America is in the heart: A personal history.* Seattle, WA: University of Washington Press.

Bulosan, C. (2005). *All the conspirators.* Seattle, WA: University of Washington Press.

Butler, J. (1990). *Gender trouble: Feminism and the subversion of identity.* New York: Routledge.

Butler, J. (1993). *Bodies that matter: On the discursive limits of sex.* New York: Routledge.

Campano, G. (2007). *Immigrant students and literacy: Reading, writing, and remembering.* New York: Teachers College Press.

Campano, G. (2009). "There are people down here": Teacher research as a collective struggle for humanization. In M. Cochran-Smith & S. Lytle (Eds.), *Inquiry as stance: Practitioner research in the next generation* (pp. 335–340). New York: Teachers College Press.

Campano, H. G. (2006). In closing: Teaching for global conversations. *Language Arts, 81*(2), 205.

Carini, P. (2001). *Starting strong: A different look at children, schools, and standards.* New York: Teachers College Press.

Carr, M. (2001). *Assessment in early childhood settings.* London: Paul Chapman.

Carr, M. (2008). Can assessment unlock and open doors to resourcefulness and agency? In S. Swaffield (Ed.), *Unlocking assessment: Understanding for reflection and application* (pp. 36–54). New York: Routledge

Carter, S. P. (2001). *The possibilities of silence: Adolescent African American female cultural identity in secondary English classrooms.* Unpublished doctoral dissertation, Vanderbilt University, Nashville, Tennessee.

Cashin, S. (2004). *The failures of integration: How race and class are undermining the American Dream.* New York: PublicAffairs.

Center for Social Media. (2008). *Code of best practices in fair use for media literacy education*. Washington, DC: American University School of Communication.

Chang, J. (2005). *Can't stop won't stop: A history of the hip-hop generation*. New York: Picador.

Chang, J. (2007). *Total chaos: The art and aesthetics of hip-hop*. New York: Basic Civitus Books.

Christensen, L. (2000). *Reading, writing, and rising up: Teaching about social justice and the power of the written word*. Milwaukee, WI: Rethinking Schools.

Cochran-Smith, M., & Lytle, S. L. (2009). *Inquiry as stance: The next generation of practitioner inquiry*. New York: Teachers College Press.

Cole, M. (1996). *Cultural psychology, a once and future discipline*. Cambridge, MA: Belknap Press of Harvard University Press.

Connor, C. (2006, September 14). *Keynote address: Assessment for learning*. Mantle of the Expert Conference, Stansted, Essex, England.

Corio, J., Knobel, M., Lankshear, D., & Leu, D. (Eds.). (2008). *Handbook of research on new literacies*. New York: Erlbaum.

Cormany, D. (2009). The name says DigME—and they do. *University of Minnesota News*. Retrieved April 7, 2009, from http://www1.umn.edu/news/features/UR_CONTENT_097501.html

Cutter, M. J. (1996). Dismantling "The Master's House": Critical literacy in Harriet Jacobs' *Incidents in the Life of a Slave Girl*. *Callaloo, 19*(1), 209–225.

Daly, G. (2004). Life on the screen: Visual literacy in education. *Edutopia, 1*(1). Retrieved June 20, 2009, from http://www.edutopia.org/life-screen

Dimarco, J. (2006). *Web portfolio design and applications*. Hershey, PA: Idea Group.

Douglass, F. (1986). *Narrative of the life of Frederick Douglass: An American slave*. New York: Penguin.

Downes, S. (2007). What connectivism is. Retrieved January 10, 2009, from http://halfanhour.blogspot.com/2007/02/what-connectivism-is.html

Dozier, C., Johnston, P., & Rogers, R. (2005). *Critical literacy/critical teaching: Tools for preparing responsive teachers*. New York: Teachers College Press.

Duncan-Andrade, J., & Morell, E. (2005). Turn up that radio teacher: Popular culture pedagogy in new century urban schools. *Journal of School Leadership, 15*(3), 285–304.

Dyson, A. H. (2005). Crafting "the humble prose of living": Rethinking oral/written relations in the echoes of spoken word. *English Education, 37*(2), 149–164.

Dyson, A. H., & Genishi, C. (Eds.). (1994). *The need for story: Cultural diversity and classroom community*. Urbana, IL: National Council of Teachers of English.

Edmiston, B. (1998). Drama as inquiry. In J. Wilhelm & B. Edmiston (Eds.), *Imagining to learn: Inquiry, ethics, and integration through drama* (pp. 25–48). Portsmouth, NH: Heinemann.

Edmiston, B. (2008). *Forming ethical identities in early childhood play*. London & New York: Routledge.

Edmiston, B., & Enciso, P. (2003). Reflections and refractions of meaning: Dialogic approaches to classroom drama and reading. In Flood, J., Lapp, D., Squire,

J., & Jensen, J. (Eds.), *The handbook of research on teaching and the English language arts* (pp. 868–880). New York: Routledge.

Elbow, P. (1973). *Writing without teachers*. New York: Oxford University Press.

Elbow, P. (2007). Reconsiderations: Voice in writing again: Embracing contraries. *College English, 70*(2), 168–188.

Engestrom, Y. (1987). *Learning by expanding: An activity theoretical approach to developmental research*. Helsinki, Finland: Orienta-Konsultit.

Feelings, M. (1992). *Jambo means hello: Swahili alphabet book*. New York: Puffin.

Fisher, M. T. (2005). From the coffee house to the school house: The promise and potential of spoken word poetry in school contexts. *English Education, 37*(2), 115–131.

Fisher, M. T. (2007). *Writing in rhythm: Spoken word poetry in urban classrooms*. New York: Teachers College Press.

Flower, L. (2008). *Community literacy and the rhetoric of public engagement*. Carbondale: Southern Illinois University Press.

Foucault, M. (1980). *Power/knowledge: Selected interviews and other writings, 1972–1977*. New York: Pantheon.

Freire, P. (2000). *Pedagogy of the oppressed* (M. Bergman Ramos, Trans.). New York: Continuum. (Original work published 1970)

Freire, P., & Macedo, D. (Eds.). (1987). *Literacy: Reading the word and the world*. South Hadley, MA: Bergin and Garvey.

Gadsden, V. L., Davis, J. E., & Artiles, A. J. (Eds.). (2009). Risk, equity, and schooling: Transforming the discourse. *Review of Research in Education, 33*, vii–xi.

Gee, J. P. (1996). *Social linguistics and literacies: Ideology in discourses* (2nd ed.). London: Taylor & Francis.

Gee, J. P. (2004). *Situated language and learning: A critique of traditional schooling*. New York: Routledge.

Goffman, E. (1959). *The presentation of self in everyday life*. New York: Anchor.

Golding, W. G. (1959). *Lord of the flies*. New York: Perigee Books.

Gonzalez, N., Moll, L. C., & Amanti. C. (Eds.). (2005). *Theorizing practices in households, communities, and classrooms*. New York: Routledge.

González Viaña, E. (2000). *Los sueños de América*. Lima, Peru: Santillana.

Greene, M. (1996). *Releasing the imagination: Essays on education, the arts, and social change*. San Francisco: Jossey-Bass.

Grimes, N. (2003). *Bronx masquerade*. New York: Puffin.

Gutiérrez, K. D. (2008). Developing a sociocritical literacy in the Third Space. *Reading Research Quarterly, 43*(2), 148–164.

Gutiérrez, K., Baquedano-López, P., & Turner, M. (1997). Putting language back into language arts: When the radical middle meets the third space. *Language Arts, 74*(5), 368–378.

Hampton, J. (Director) (1987). *Eyes on the prize* [Motion picture]. United States: Blackside Productions.

Hanh, T. N., & Berrigan, D. (2000). *The raft is not the shore: Conversations toward a Buddhist/Christian awareness*. Maryknoll, NY: Orbis Books.

Harris, J. (2006). *Rewriting: How to do things with texts*. Logan, UT: Utah State University Press.

Harste, J. C. (2001). What education as inquiry is and isn't. In S. Boran & B. Comber (Eds.), *Critiquing whole language and curriculum inquiry* (pp. 1–17). Urbana, IL: National Council of Teachers of English.

Heath, S. B. (1983). *Ways with words: Language, life, and work in communities and classrooms*. Cambridge, UK: Cambridge University Press.

Heath, S. B., & Wolf, S. (2005). *Dramatic learning in the primary school*. London: Creative Partnerships.

Heathcote, D. (1984). Dramatic activity. In L. Johnston & C. O'Neill (Eds.), *Dorothy Heathcote: Collected writings on drama and education* (pp. 54–60). London: Hutchinson.

Heathcote, D. (2006). Foreword. In J. Carroll, M. Anderson, & D. Cameron (Eds.), *Real players? Drama, technology, and education*, (pp. v–ix). Stoke-on-Trent: Trentham.

Heathcote, D., & Bolton, G. (1995). *Drama for learning: Dorothy Heathcote's Mantle of the Expert approach to education*. Portsmouth, NH: Heinemann.

Hill, M. L. (2009). Wounded healing: Forming a storytelling community in hip-hop lit. *Teachers College Record, 111*(1), 248–293.

Holland, D., Lachicotte, W., Skinner, D., & Cain, C. (1998). *Identity and agency in cultural worlds*. Cambridge, MA: Harvard University Press.

hooks, b. (2003). *Teaching community: A pedagogy of hope*. London & New York: Routledge.

Housen, A. (2007). Art viewing and aesthetic development: Designing for the viewer. In P. Villeneuve (Ed.), *From periphery to center: Art museum education in the 21st century* (pp. 102–134). Reston, VA: The National Art Education Association.

Hurston, Z. N. (1991). *Their eyes were watching God*. Urbana, IL: University of Illinois Press. (Original work published 1937)

James, M., Black, P., Carmichael, P., Conner, C., Dudley, P., Fox, A., et al. (2006). *Learning how to learn: Tools for schools*. New York: Routledge.

Jenkins, H. (2006). *Confronting the challenges of participatory culture: Media education for the 21st century*. Chicago: MacArthur Foundation.

Jimenez, F. (1999). *The circuit*. New York: Houghton Mifflin.

Jocson, K. M. (2005). "Taking it to the mic": Pedagogy of *June Jordan's poetry for the people* and partnership with an urban high school. *English Education, 37*(2), 132–148.

Jordan, J. (1995). *June Jordan's poetry for the people: A revolutionary blueprint*. New York: Routledge.

Kelly, I. (2008). The forgotten ones. *The Viking, 1*(3), 32–38.

Kent, T. (1993). *Paralogic rhetoric*. London: Associated University Press.

Kinloch, V. (2005). Poetry, literacy, and creativity: Fostering effective learning strategies in an urban classroom. *English Education, 37*(2), 96–114.

Knobel, M. (1999). *Everyday literacies*. New York: Peter Lang.

Kress, G. (2003). *Literacy in the new media age*. New York: Routledge.

Lankshear, C., & Knobel, M. (2006). *New literacies: Everyday practices and classroom learning* (2nd ed.). Maidenhead, UK: Open University Press.

Lapsley, M. (October 28, 2008). Presentation: "Forgiveness and healing: A South African perspective." St. Paul, MN: Bethel College.

Leander, K. M. (2009). Composing with old and new media: Toward a parallel pedagogy. In V. Carrington & M. Robinson (Eds.), *Digital literacies: Social learning and classroom practices* (pp. 147–163). Los Angeles: Sage.

Leander, K., & Sheehy, M. (Eds.). (2004). *Spatializing literacy research and practice*. New York: Peter Lang.

Lee, A. (Director). (2005). *Brokeback mountain* [Motion picture]. United States: Paramount Pictures.

Lee, C. D. (2007). *The role of culture in academic literacies: Conducting our blooming in the midst of the whirlwind*. New York: Teachers College Press.

Lee, H. (2002). *To kill a mockingbird*. New York: Harper. (Original work published 1960)

Lefebvre, H. (1991). *The production of space*. Cambridge, MA: Blackwell.

Lenhart, A., Arafeh, S., Smith, A., & Macgill, A. R. (2008). *Writing, technology, and teens*. Washington, DC: Pew Charitable Trusts. Retrieved June 15, 2009 from http://www.pewinternet.org/~/media//Files/Reports/2008/PIP_Writing_Report_FINAL3.pdf

Lerman, L., & Borstel, J. (2007). Liz Lerman's critical response process: The core steps and an interview with Liz Lerman. *Contact Quarterly, 33*(1), 16–24.

Lewis, J. (2008). 3rd generation assessment in a primary classroom. Retrieved April 6, 2009, from http://www.mantleoftheexpert.com/about-moe/articles/

Lewison, M., Leland. C., & Harste, J. (2008). *Creating critical classrooms: K–8 reading and writing with an edge*. New York: Erlbaum.

Lorde, A. (2007). *Sister outsider: The essays and speeches of Audre Lorde*. Berkeley, CA: Crossing Press.

Luke, A., & Freebody, P. (1997). Shaping the social practices of reading. In S. Muspratt, A. Luke, & P. Freebody (Eds.), *Constructing critical literacies: Teaching and learning textual practice* (pp. 185–225). Cresskill, NJ: Hampton Press.

Lyon, G. E. (1996). Where I'm from. In J. Blum, B. Holman, & M. Pellington (Eds.), *The United States of poetry* (p. 24). New York: Harry N. Adams.

Mahiri, J., Ali, M., Scott, A. L., Asmerom, B., & Ayers, R. (2008). Both sides of the mic: Community literacies in the age of hip hop. In J. Flood, S. B. Heath, & D. Lapp (Eds.)., *Handbook of research on teaching literacy through communicative and visual arts* (Vol. 2) (pp. 279–287). New York: Taylor & Francis.

Marcus, H., & Nurius, P. (1986). Possible selves: The interface between motivation and the self-concept. In K. Yardley & T. Holness (Eds.) *Self and identity: Psychosocial perspectives* (pp. 157–172). Chichester, NY: Wiley.

Medina, C., & Campano, G. (2007). Performing identities through drama and teatro practices in multilingual classrooms. *Language Arts, 83*(4), 332–341.

Meyer, S. (2006). *Twilight*. New York: Little, Brown.

Mills, M. (2009). *Introducing survival and event history analysis*. Thousand Oaks, CA: Sage.

Misson, R., & Morgan, W. (2006). *Critical literacy and the aesthetic: Transforming the English classroom*. Urbana, IL: National Council of Teachers of English.

Mohanty, S. (1997). *Literary theory and the claims of history: Postmodernism, objectivity, multicultural politics*. New York: Simon & Schuster Macmillan.

Morrell, E. (2008). *Critical literacy and urban youth: Pedagogies of access, dissent, and liberation*. New York: Routledge.

Morrison, T. (1994). *The Nobel lecture in literature, 1993*. New York: Knopf.

Moya, P. (2001). *Learning from experience: Minority identities, multicultural struggles*. Berkeley: University of California Press.

Mueller, J. (2008). Authentic assessment toolbox. Retrieved March 18, 2009, from http://jonathan.mueller.faculty.noctrl.edu/toolbox/portfolios.htm

Ohler, J. B. (2007). *Digital storytelling in the classroom: New media pathways to literacy, learning, and creativity*. Thousand Oaks, CA: Corwin Press.

Omar, W. (2008). From storytelling to community development, Jaghori, Afghanistan. In R. Solinger, M. Fox, & K. Irani, (Eds.), *Telling stories to change the world: Global voices on the power of narrative to build community and make social justice claims* (pp. 193–200). New York: Routledge.

O'Neill, C. (1995). *Drama worlds: A framework for process drama*. Portsmouth, NH: Heinemann.

Ong, W. (1982). *Orality and literacy: The technologizing of the word*. London: Methuen.

Orwell, G. (1948). Politics and the English language. In J. D. McCallum (Ed.), *The college omnibus* (6th ed.) (pp. 63–72). New York: Harcourt, Brace.

Osei-Kofi, N. (2005). Pathologizing the poor: A framework for understanding Ruby Paine's work. *Equity & Excellence in Education, 38*(4), 367–375.

Perez, A. I. (2002). *My diary from here to there: Mi diario de aqui hasta alla*. New York: Children's Book Press.

Pratt, M. L. (1991). Arts of the contact zone. *Profession 91*, 33–40. New York: Modern Language Association.

Richardson, W. (2009). *Blogs, wikis, podcasts, and other powerful web tools for classrooms*. Thousand Oaks, CA: Corwin Press.

Robinson, K. (2001). *Out of our minds: Learning to be creative*. New York: Capstone.

Robinson, C., & Taylor, C. (2007). Theorizing student voice: values and perspectives. *Improving Schools, 10*(1), 5–17.

Rosaldo, R. (1993). *Culture and truth: The remaking of social analysis*. Boston: Beacon Press.

Rozema, R., & Webb, A. (2008). *Literature and the Web: Reading and responding with new technologies*. Portsmouth, NH: Heinemann.

Samuels, D. (April 4, 2006). Presentation: "Go light the world." Minneapolis, MN: Westminister Presbyterian Church.

Sánchez-Casal, S., & Macdonald, A. (Eds.) (2002). *Twenty-first century feminist classrooms: Pedagogies of identity and difference.* New York: Macmillan.

Sannino, A., Daniels, H., & Gutiérrez, K. (Eds.). (2009). *Learning and expanding with activity theory.* New York: Cambridge University Press.

Santiago, E. (2006). *When I was Puerto Rican.* Cambridge, MA: Da Capo Press.

Scardamalia, M. (2002). Collective cognitive responsibility for the advancement of knowledge. Retrieved March 21, 2009, from http://ikit.org/fulltext/2002CollectiveCog.pdf

Schneider, J., Crumpler, T., & Rogers, T. (2006). *Process drama and multiple literacies: Addressing social, cultural, and ethical issues.* Portsmouth, NH: Heinemann.

Scott Nixon, A. (2009). Mediating social thought through digital storytelling. *Pedagogies: An International Journal, 4*(1), 63–76.

Shaffer, D. (2006). *How computer games help children learn.* New York: Palgrave Macmillan.

Shange, N. (1977). *For colored girls who have considered suicide/when the rainbow is enuf.* New York: Scribner.

Shirky, C. (2009). *Here comes everybody: The power of organizing without organizations.* New York: Penguin.

Siemens, G. (2008). The unique ideas in connectivism. Retrieved March 2, 2009, from http://connectivism.ca/blog/2008/08/what_is_the_unique_idea_in_con.html

Soja, E. (1996). *Thirdspace: Journeys to Los Angeles and other real-and-imagined places.* Cambridge, MA: Blackwell.

Solinger, R., Fox, M., & Irani, K. (Eds.). (2008). *Telling stories to change the world: Global voices on the power of narrative to build community and make social justice claims.* New York: Routledge.

Sontag, S. (2002). *On photography.* New York: Penguin.

Sontag, S. (2008). *Reborn: Journals and notebooks 1947–1964.* New York: Farrar, Straus and Giroux.

Stafford, W. (1998). Ritual to read to each other. In *The way it is: New and selected poems* (p. 75). St. Paul, MN: Graywolf Press.

Street, B. (1984). *Literacy in theory and practice.* Cambridge, UK: Cambridge University Press.

Street, B. (1995). *Social literacies: Critical approaches to literacy in development, ethnography, and education.* London: Longman.

Sunstein, B. S., & Chiseri-Strater, E. (2007). *FieldWorking: Reading and writing research* (3rd ed.). Boston: Bedford/St. Martin's.

Swaffield, S. (Ed.). (2008). *Unlocking assessment: Understanding for reflection and application.* New York: Routledge

Taylor, D. (1996). *Toxic literacies: Exposing the injustices of bureaucratic texts.* Portsmouth, NH: Heinemann.

Teuton, S. K. (2008). *Red land, red power: Grounding knowledge in the American Indian novel.* Durham, NC: Duke University Press.

Tutu, D. (1999). *No future without forgiveness.* New York: Doubleday.

Van Sant, G. (Director). (2008). *Milk* [Motion picture]. United States: Focus Features.

Vasudevan, L. (2006). Looking for angels: Knowing adolescents by engaging with their multimodal literacy practices. *Journal of Adolescent and Adult Literacy, 50*(4), 252–256.

Velez-Ibanez, C., & Greenberg, J. (1992). Formation and transformation of funds of knowledge among U.S. Mexican households. *Anthropology and Education Quarterly, 23*(4), 313–335.

Vygotsky, L. (1967) Play and its role in the mental development of the child. *Soviet Psychology, 5*, 6–18.

Wagner, B. J. (1998). *Educational drama and language arts: What research shows.* Portsmouth, NH: Heinemann.

Walcott, D. (1998). Interview. In G. Plimpton (Ed.), *Writers at work: The Paris Review interviews*, 8th series (pp. 2–23). New York: Penguin.

Weis, L., & Fine, M. (2000). *Construction sites: Excavating race, class, and gender among urban youth.* New York: Teachers College Press.

Weiss, J., & Herndon, S. (2001). *Brave new voices: The youth speaks guide to teaching spoken word poetry.* Portsmouth, NH: Heinemann.

Wells, G. (1999). *Learning for life in the 21st century.* New York: John Wiley.

Wenger, E. (1998). *Communities of practice: Learning, meaning and identity.* New York: Cambridge University Press.

Wertsch, J. (1998). *Mind as action.* New York: Oxford University Press.

Wesch, M. (2009). From knowledgable to knowledge-able: learning in new media environments. Retrieved June 30, 2009 from http://www.academiccommons.org/commons/essay/knowledgable-knowledge-able

Wiggins, G., & McTighe, J. (2005). *Understanding by design* (2nd ed.). Upper Saddle River, NJ: Prentice Hall.

Wilhelm, D. (2005). *The revealers.* New York: Farrar, Straus and Giroux.

Wissman, K. (2009). Reading and becoming living authors: Urban girls pursuing a poetry of self-definition. *English Journal, 98*(3), 39–45.

Wohlwend, K. (2008). Play as a literacy of possibilities: Expanding meanings in practices, materials, and spaces. *Language Arts, 86*(2), 127–136.

Wortham, S. (2005). Socialization beyond the speech event. *Journal of Linguistic Anthropology, 15*(1), 95–112.

Yeats, W. B. (1889). The stolen child. In *The wanderings of Oisin and other poems.* London: Kegan Paul, Trench & Company.

Young, V. A. (2007). *Your average nigga: Performing race, literacy, and masculinity.* Detroit, MI: Wayne State University Press.

Index

About the Authors

Richard Beach is professor of English education at the University of Minnesota. He is the author or co-author of *Teaching Writing Using Blogs, Wikis, and Other Digital Tools; Teaching Literature to Adolescents; Teachingmedialiteracy.com: A Web-Based Guide to Links and Activities; Inquiry-Based English Instruction: Engaging Students in Literature and Life;* and *High School Students' Competing Social Worlds: Negotiating Identities and Allegiances through Responding to Multicultural Literature.* He is also the organizing editor for the annual "Annotated Bibliography of Research" for *Research in the Teaching of English.* He is a member of the National Council of Teachers of English (NCTE) Commission on Media and was awarded the 2009 Computers in Reading Research Award from the International Reading Association (IRA).

Gerald Campano was a full-time classroom teacher in Houston, Puerto Rico, and California's Central Valley and has worked with adult English language learners in North Philadelphia. He is currently an associate professor at Indiana University, Bloomington. His research interests and publications address (im)migrant identities in the contexts of schooling, urban education, Filipina American studies, and practitioner inquiry. Throughout his work, he has been committed to creating opportunities for students to mobilize their identities and rich cultural resources in the elementary literacy curriculum. Gerald is a Carnegie Scholar and the author of *Immigrant Students and Literacy: Reading, Writing, and Remembering,* for which he received the 2009 David H. Russell Research Award from NCTE.

Brian Edmiston is associate professor of teaching and learning at The Ohio State University, where he teaches courses in dramatic inquiry. He is the co-author of *Imagining to Learn: Inquiry, Ethics,* and *Integration through Drama,* and the author of *Forming Ethical Identities in Early Childhood Play.* At Ohio State he co-directed the Martha King Center for

Language and Literacies, and recently received a Distinguished Teaching Award. A recipient of the American Alliance of Theatre and Education's Outstanding Research Award, he is also a member of the NCTE Standing Committee on Research.

Melissa Borgmann has worked as a high school English teacher in the Minneapolis Public Schools, a literacy coach through the Perpich Center for Arts Education, a K–12 teaching artist, and director of The Juno Collective, an organization centered on literacy and leadership in and through the arts. In 2007, her Juno programs, including Teens Rock the Mic, were selected by Harvard Project Zero for a case study looking at excellence in arts education. Melissa has also worked as a teacher-consultant for the Minnesota Writing Project, the Arts for Academic Achievement project, the Perpich Center for Arts Education, and as an advisor to the *Teaching Artist Journal* design team.